FASTER THAN LIGHT

Other Books by Marilyn Nelson

Seneca Village (2012; in manuscript)

Sweethearts of Rhythm (2009), by Marilyn Nelson,
    illustrated by Jerry Pinkney

The Freedom Business (2008), by Marilyn Nelson,
    illustrated by Deborah Dancy

*Miss Crandall's School for Young Ladies & Little Misses
    of Color* (2007), by Elizabeth Alexander and
    Marilyn Nelson, illustrated by Floyd Cooper

The Cachoeira Tales and Other Poems (2005),
    by Marilyn Nelson

A Wreath for Emmett Till (2005), by Marilyn Nelson,
    illustrated by Phillipe Lardy

Fortune's Bones: The Manumission Requiem (2004),
    by Marilyn Nelson

Carver: A Life in Poems (2001), by Marilyn Nelson

The Fields of Praise: New and Selected Poems (1997),
    by Marilyn Nelson

Magnificat (1994), by Marilyn Nelson Waniek

The Homeplace (1990), by Marilyn Nelson Waniek

Mama's Promises (1985), by Marilyn Nelson Waniek

For the Body (1978), by Marilyn Nelson Waniek

NEW AND SELECTED POEMS, 1996–2011

FASTER THAN LIGHT

MARILYN NELSON

LOUISIANA STATE UNIVERSITY PRESS

BATON ROUGE

Published by Louisiana State University Press
Copyright © 2012 by Marilyn Nelson
All rights reserved
Manufactured in the United States of America

Designer: Barbara Neely Bourgoyne
Typefaces: News Gothic and Calluna

The author gratefully acknowledges the editors of the following publications, in which some of the new poems first appeared: *African American Review:* "Millie-Christine"; *A Long and Winding Road:* "The Mohembo Road" (forthcoming); *American Arts Quarterly:* "Little Dialogue with the Muse" and "A Small Good News"; *The American Scholar:* "Nine Times Nine, on Awe"; *The Antioch Review:* "Written in Clouds"; *At Length* (atlengthmag.com): "In the Waiting Room"; *Beltway Poetry Quarterly:* "Honor Guard"; *Black Renaissance/Renaissance Noire:* "Conductor," "The Cotillion," and "Sky-Land"; *Cutthroat: A Journal of the Arts:* "Bivouac in a Storm," "Six-Minute Dogfight," and "To the Confederate Dead"; *The Hudson Review:* "For the Feast of Corpus Christi"; *Image:* "The Contemplative Life"; *The New Bread Loaf Anthology of Contemporary American Poetry:* "Live Jazz, Franklin Park Zoo"; *Obsidian II:* "First Alzheimer's Sonnet" and "Second Alzheimer's Sonnet"; *Platte Valley Review:* "Thompson and Seaman Vows, African Union Church" and "Words and Whispers"; *The Writer's Chronicle:* "Sisters of Charity."

Published collections in which selected poems have appeared:
Sweethearts of Rhythm (Dial Books, 2009)
The Freedom Business (Wordsong, 2008)
Miss Crandall's School for Young Ladies & Little Misses of Color (Wordsong, 2007)
The Cachoeira Tales and Other Poems (Louisiana State University Press, 2005)
A Wreath for Emmett Till (Houghton Mifflin, 2005)
Fortune's Bones: The Manumission Requiem (Front Street, 2004)
Carver: A Life in Poems (Front Street, 2001)

Library of Congress Cataloging-in-Publication Data
Nelson, Marilyn, 1946–
 Faster than light : new and selected poems, 1996–2011 / Marilyn Nelson.
   p. cm.
ISBN 978-0-8071-4733-7 (cloth : alk. paper) — ISBN 978-0-8071-4734-4 (pbk. : alk. paper) — ISBN 978-0-8071-4735-1 (pdf) — ISBN 978-0-8071-4736-8 (epub) — ISBN 978-0-8071-4737-5 (mobi)
 I. Title.
PS3573.A4795F37 2012
811'.54—dc23

                                                            2011051511

The paper in this book meets the guidelines for permanence and durability of the Committee on Production Guidelines for Book Longevity of the Council on Library Resources. ♾

This book is dedicated to Stephen Roxburgh,
editor, publisher, mentor, friend

Everything is made of light.

—HERACLITUS

Everything we see is light.

—PAUL CÉZANNE

You must shine your own light.

—SOJOURNER TRUTH

CONTENTS

I. LYRIC HISTORIES

A Wreath for Emmett Till   3

From *The Freedom Business*

Witness   10

Pestilence   11

A Voyage by Sea   12

Keeper of the Keys   13

Fat on the Fire   15

Meg   16

Cows in the Shade   17

Sap Rising   18

Farm Garden   19

The Freedom Business   20

From *Fortune's Bones: The Manumission Requiem*

On Abrigador Hill   21

Dinah's Lament   23

Not My Bones   24

From *Seneca Village*

Sky-Land   26

Conductor   28

The Cotillion   29

Address   30

Thompson and Seaman Vows, African Union Church   31

Words and Whispers   32

Little Box   34

Miracle in the Collection Plate   35

Sisters of Charity   37

Uncle Epiphany   38

From *Miss Crandall's School for Young Ladies & Little Misses of Color*

The Book   39

Family   40

The Tao of the Trial   41

Miss Ann Eliza Hammond   42

Etymology   43

Albert Hinkley   44

Worth   45

From *Carver: A Life in Poems*

Watkins Laundry and Apothecary   46

Old Settlers' Reunion   48

Four a.m. in the Woods   49

Cafeteria Food   50

Called   51

My People   52

Chemistry 101   53

From an Alabama Farmer   54

Bedside Reading   55

Poultry Husbandry   57

1905   59

Veil-Raisers   61

How a Dream Dies   62

The Dimensions of the Milky Way   64

Ruellia Noctiflora   65

Goliath   67

House Ways and Means   68

"God's Little Workshop"   69

Eureka   71

Mineralogy   72

Last Talk with Jim Hardwick   74

Moton Field   75

From *Sweethearts of Rhythm*

Bugle Call Rag   76

Chattanooga Choo-Choo   77

Jump, Jump, Jump   78

She's Crazy with the Heat   79

Red-Hot Mama   80

That Man of Mine   81

Improvisation, 1948   82

Drum Solo, 1950   83

The Song Is You   84

II. OTHER SELECTED POEMS

From *The Cachoeira Tales and Other Poems*

Faster Than Light   87

Cachoeira Tales   92

General Prologue   92

C.I.A.   97

Harmonia and Moreen   97

Baixa Mall   99

Olodum   105

A Igreja do Nossa Senhor do Bonfim   109

Triolets for Triolet   113

III. NEW AND UNCOLLECTED POEMS

Millie-Christine   119

A Small Good News   126

Little Dialogue with the Muse   127

First Alzheimer's Sonnet   128

Second Alzheimer's Sonnet   129

The Truceless Wars   130

Live Jazz, Franklin Park Zoo   131

To the Confederate Dead   132

Bivouac in a Storm   135

Six-Minute Dogfight   137

Written in Clouds   138

Honor Guard   139

Eternal Optimist   140

Psalm for Another People   141

Nine Times Nine, on Awe   142

In the Waiting Room   145

The Mohembo Road   148

For the Feast of Corpus Christi   152

How to Be Human Now   154

   The Contemplative Life   154

   The Language of the Absolute   155

   Stone Adze   156

   The Risk Unto Death   157

   Truth and Beauty   157

   La Gare Central   157

   Where Humanity Begins   157

   Nothing Stranger   158

From "Adventure-Monk!"   159

I. LYRIC HISTORIES

A Wreath for Emmett Till

R.I.P. Emmett Louis Till, 1941–1955

Color

light/shall

I

Rosemary for remembrance, Shakespeare wrote:
a speech for poor Ophelia, who went mad
when her love killed her father. Flowers had
a language then. Rose petals in a note
said, *I love you;* a sheaf of bearded oat
said, *Your music enchants me.* Goldenrod:
Be careful. Weeping-willow twigs: *I'm sad.*
What should my wreath for Emmett Till denote?
First, heliotrope, for *Justice shall be done.*
Daisies and white lilacs, for *Innocence.*
Then mandrake: *Horror* (wearing a white hood,
or bare-faced, laughing). For grief, more than one,
for one is not enough: rue, yew, cypress.
Forget-me-nots. Though if I could, I would.

II

Forget him not. Though if I could, I would
forget much of that racial memory.
No: I remember, like a haunted tree
set off from other trees in the wildwood
by one bare bough. If trees could speak, it could
describe, in words beyond words, make us see
the strange fruit that still ghosts its reverie,
misty companion of its solitude.
Dendrochronology could give its age
in centuries, by counting annual rings:
seasons of drought and rain. But one night, blood,
spilled at its roots, blighted its foliage.
Pith outward, it has been slowly dying,
pierced by the screams of a shortened childhood.

Tree,
roses

III

Pierced by the screams of a shortened childhood,
my heartwood has been scarred for fifty years
by what I heard, with hundreds of green ears.
That jackal laughter. Two hundred years I stood
listening to small struggles to find food,
to the songs of creature life, which disappears
and comes again, to the music of the spheres.
Two hundred years of deaths I understood.
Then slaughter axed one quiet summer night,
shivering the deep silence of the stars.
A running boy, five men in close pursuit.
One dark, five pale faces in the moonlight.
Noise, silence, back-slaps. One match, five cigars.
Emmett Till's name still catches in the throat.

IV

Emmett Till's name still catches in my throat,
like syllables waylaid in a stutterer's mouth.
A fourteen-year old stutterer, in the South
to visit relatives, and to be taught
the family's ways. His mother had finally bought
that White Sox cap; she'd made him swear an oath
to be careful around white folks. She'd told him the truth
of many a Mississippi anecdote:
Some white folks have blind souls. In his suitcase
she'd packed dungarees, T-shirts, underwear,
and comic books. She'd given him a note
for the conductor, waved to his chubby face,
wondered if he'd remember to brush his hair.
Her only child. A body left to bloat.

V

Your only child, a body thrown to bloat,
mother of sorrows, of justice denied.
Surely you must have thought of suicide,

seeing his gray flesh, chains around his throat.
Surely you didn't know you would devote
the rest of your changed life to dignified
public remembrance of how Emmett died,
innocence slaughtered by the hands of hate.
If sudden loving light proclaimed you blest
would you bow your head in humility,
your healed heart overflow with gratitude?
Would you say yes, like the mother of Christ?
Or would you say no to your destiny,
mother of a boy martyr, if you could?

VI

Mutilated boy martyr, if I could,
I'd put you in a parallel universe,
give you a better fate. There is none worse.
I'd let you live through a happy boyhood,
let your gifts bloom into a livelihood
on a planet that didn't bear Cain's curse.
I'd put you in a nice, safe universe,
not like this one. A universe where you'd
surpass your mother's dreams. But parallel
realities may have terrorists, too.
Evil multiplies to infinitude,
like mirrors facing each other in hell.
You were a wormhole history passed through,
transformed by the memory of your victimhood.

VII

Erase the memory of Emmett's victimhood.
Let's write the obituary of a life
lived well and wisely, mourned by a loving wife
or partner, friends, and a vast multitude.
Remember the high purpose he pursued.
Remember how he earned a nation's grief.
Remember accomplishments beyond belief,

5

honors enough to make us ooh, slack-jawed,
as if we looked up at a meteor shower
or were children watching a fireworks display.
Let America remember what he taught.
Or at least let him die in a World Trade Tower ~ Sonet 6 (terrists)
rescuing others, that unforgettable day,
that memory of monsters, that bleak thought.

VIII   a/is

The memory of monsters: That bleak thought
should be confined to a horror-movie world.
A horror classic, in which a blind girl
hears, one by one, the windows broken out,
an ax at the front door. In the onslaught
of terror, as a hate-filled body hurls
itself against her door, her senses swirl
around one prayer: Please, God, forget me not.
The body-snatchers jiggle the doorknob,
werewolves and vampires slaver after blood,
the circus of nightmares is here. She screams,
he screams, neighbors with names he knows, a mob
heartless and heedless, answering to no god,
tears through the patchwork drapery of our dreams.

IX

KKK   Imagery

Tears, through the patchwork drapery of dream,
for the hanging bodies, the men on flaming pyres,
the crowds standing around like devil choirs,
the children's eyes lit by the fire's gleams
filled with the delight of licking ice cream,
men who hear hog screams as a man expires,
watch-fob good-luck charms teeth pulled out with pliers,
sinners I can't believe Christ's death redeems, ~ Christ died for this
your ash hair, Shulamith—Emmett, your eye,
machetes, piles of shoes, bulldozed mass graves,
the broken towers, the air filled with last breaths,

6

the blasphemies pronounced to justify
the profane, obscene theft of human lives.
Let me gather spring flowers for a wreath.

all of a sudn poem is positive

X

Let me gather spring flowers for a wreath.
Not lilacs from the dooryard, but wildflowers
I'd search for in the greening woods for hours
of solitude, meditating on death.
Let me wander through pathless woods, beneath
the choirs of small birds trumpeting their powers
at the intruder trampling through their bowers,
disturbing their peace. I cling to the faith
that innocence lives on, that a blind soul
can see again. That miracles do exist.
In my house, there is still something called grace, *religion*
which melts ice shards of hate and makes hearts whole.
I bear armloads of flowers home, to twist
into a circle: trillium, Queen Anne's lace . . . — *more flowers*

XI

Trillium, apple-blossoms, Queen Anne's lace,
woven with oak twigs, for sincerity . . .
Thousands of oak trees around this country
groaned with the weight of men slain for their race,
their murderers acquitted in almost every case.
One night five black men died on the same tree,
with toeless feet, in this Land of the Free.
This country we love has a Janus face:
One mouth speaks with forked tongue, the other reads
the Constitution. My country, 'tis of both
thy nightmare history and thy grand dream,
thy centuries of good and evil deeds,
I sing. Thy fruited plain, thy undergrowth
of mandrake, which flowers white as moonbeams.

7

XII

Indian pipe, bloodroot. White as moonbeams,
their flowers. Picked, one blackens, and one bleeds
a thick red sap. Indian pipe, a weed
which thrives on rot, is held in disesteem,
though it does have its use in nature's scheme,
unlike the rose. The bloodroot poppy needs
no explanation here: Its red sap pleads
the case for its inclusion in the theme
of a wreath for the memory of Emmett Till.
Though the white poppy means *forgetfulness,*
who could forget, when red sap on a wreath
recalls the brown boy five white monsters killed?
Forgetting would call for consciencelessness.
Like the full moon, which smiled calmly on his death.

XIII

Like the full moon, which smiled calmly on his death.
Like the stars, which fluttered their quicksilver wings.
Like the unbroken song creation sings
while humankind tramples the grapes of wrath.
Like wildflowers growing beside the path
a boy was dragged along, blood spattering
their white petals as he, abandoning
all hope, gasped his agonizing last breath.
Like a nation sending its children off to fight
our faceless enemy, immortal fear,
the most feared enemy of the human race.
Like a plague of not knowing wrong from right.
Like the consciencelessness of the atmosphere.
Like a gouged eye, watching boots kick a face.

XIV

Like his gouged eye, which watched boots kick his face,
we must bear witness to atrocity.
But we are whole: We can speak what we see.

People may disappear, leaving no trace,
unless we stand before the populace,
orators denouncing the slavery
to fear. For the lynchers feared the lynchee,
what he might do, being of another race,
a great unknown. They feared because they saw
their own inner shadows, their vicious dreams,
the farthest horizons of their own thought,
their jungles immune to the rule of law.
We can speak now, or bear unforgettable shame.
Rosemary for remembrance, Shakespeare wrote.

XV

Rosemary for remembrance, Shakespeare wrote.
If I could forget, believe me, I would.
Pierced by the screams of a shortened childhood,

Emmett Till's name still catches in my throat.
Mamie's one child, a body thrown to bloat,
Mutilated boy martyr. If I could
Erase the memory of Emmett's victimhood,
The memory of monsters . . . That bleak thought
Tears through the patchwork drapery of dreams.

Let me gather spring flowers for a wreath:

Trillium, apple-blossoms, Queen Anne's lace,
Indian-pipe, bloodroot, white as moonbeams,
Like the full moon which smiled calmly on his death,
Like his gouged eye, which watched boots kick his face.

9

From *The Freedom Business*

Based on the 1798 narrative of Venture Smith, born in Guinea ca. 1729. Smith's narrative documents his capture by slave traders, his three decades as a slave in America, and his eventual purchase of his own freedom and that of his wife and children.

WITNESS

"My Father Named Me Broteer"

I was the first wife's firstborn of the Prince
of Dukandarra. My father was wise and strong,
a just and moderate ruler, a true king.
His name—Saungm Furro—was his only bond.
When he stood in a crowd of countrymen
(each taller, broader across shoulders and chest
than your average white man, and mahogany brown),
my father towered over most of the rest,
draped in his elegant toga of kente cloth.
When he sat, he sat on The Golden Stool.
I still remember his rumbling voice, his laugh.

(Hidden with my mother in the bushes,
      I would see him killed.)

10

PESTILENCE

Six thousand men strong, the army poured toward the sea.
Slavery's wide wings gliding overhead
spread an infecting shadow as, step by step,
they swept like a battalion of ravenous ants,
advancing through the landscape and leaving a stench
drenched in sweat, shit, vomit, terror, and smoke.
The gentlefolk of every village burned,
borne by the black tide, shuffled in the slavers' wake,
awake for the first time to a larger fate,
indeterminate but nasty: on the world stage
in an age when a workforce could be bought and sold.
Golden, the flow of human life down the green slopes.
Hopes shriveled in the glare of the distant bright
whitewashed castle's acrid glitter in sunlight.

A VOYAGE BY SEA

(1738)

Eleven months on the *Charming Susanna*.
"An ordinary passage." But smallpox
amok in the hold set sixty people free. *slave trade - death sets them*
The sea gulped them down in a boil of grins and fins, *free*
men and women tossed like offal to the sharks.

Simile

Discharge excretion diarrhea spew
oozing pustular nausea vomit snot

Brought from Africa, they were to be sold to the New World
as fuel for the grinding machines of history. *metaphor*

Simile

Festering sticky shit-smeared mucus pus
pissed-on menstruating sweaty stinking

                                Dazed
and erased en route before they were renamed
by whim, who were those anonymous, generic slaves,
graveless as garbage, splashed to the greedy waves?

alliteration

Simile

KEEPER OF THE KEYS

(1740)

What makes a man a man is his good name:
the rest of it is beyond our control.
Trustworthiness and honor are riches
no one can steal. Let men have faith in you:
hold true to your promise. My father's values
were my sum and substance during that cocoon year.

From freedom to a new world was one year
of grief, shock, sorrow, and learning my new name
and Master's language. But not Master's values:
here, at least, was something I could control.
Here, there was a true, essential *I*
which only I could own. Here were my riches.

In Barbados, the surviving unpurchased riches
were barbered, washed, and oiled. After a year
of misery and homeward yearning, they
were marched to market, sold, and given new names,
their present strength and their futures under white control,
their traditional beliefs toppled under Christian values.

I was nine years old, and filled with my father's values,
when we reached Rhode Island. From there my master's riches
sailed to his home, his keys under my control,
while he disembarked for business. For a year
I had practiced *Become True Virtue. Bring Honor to Your Name.*
Now I promised my master his keys would be safe with me.

At Master's home, his father ordered me
to give him the keys, as there were some things of value
among Master's things, which were purchased in his name.
I told him my master had trusted me with his riches;
I had promised to keep them safe. After a year
of becoming, I emerged. I took control.

13

My master's father threatened, but I controlled
the keys, concealed in my shirt, or under me
while I slept, more watchfully than I'd slept all year.
When at last my master unpacked his things of value,
he told his father he would trust me with all of his riches,
because, where I come from, a man is as good as his name.

What value has a man, beyond his name?
Can he control his fate? Know his death year?
He is richest whose honor outlives him.

FAT ON THE FIRE

(ca. 1756)

I was sold to a Thomas Stanton of Stonington,
and parted from my Meg and our newborn
(our first, our Hannah). I carried a saved sum—
two thousand coppers and ten silver coins,
amounting to twenty-one pounds—rolled in my coat.
My master's brother borrowed my savings of me,
first giving me his signed I.O.U. note.
It took a year to get Master to agree
to purchase Meg and Hannah (seven hundred pounds).
Hannah's a feisty, curious little imp.
She walked at ten months; now she's running around
sticking little brown fingers into everything.

Today, a caterwaul called me from the barn
to find the source of a blood-curdling screech.
Instead of marauders bent on doing harm,
I found Mistress promising Meg she'd teach
her to let that damned pup spoil her nap.
All three of them were screaming like mad seagulls,
and Mistress was striking Meg with her horsewhip.
Now I've gone and done something that breaks all of their rules—
my master will probably sell me to the first buyer;
I might as well kiss my loaned life savings farewell—
I seized that whip and hurled it on the fire.
It sizzled like a slave-owner's soul in hell.

MEG

after Leopold Senghor

My love, rest your soothing hands on my brow, your fingers smooth as
   velvet fur.
Above us, the listing trees barely rustle in the high night's breath.
No sound of lullaby.
Let this rhythmic silence hold us.

Let us listen to its music, listen to our drumming, dark blood; listen
to the deep pulse of Africa beating in forgotten villages.
Weary, the moon gropes her way toward her bed in the sea.
Now scattered laughter grows sleepy; even the storytellers
nod like babies tied on their mothers' backs.
Now the dancers' feet grow heavy, and leaden the chorus of call and response.
This is the hour of stars and of the night, dreaming
where she lies on a hill of clouds, wrapped in a length of milky-way cloth.
The thatched roofs gleam tenderly. What do they whisper to the stars?
Inside, the fires die among familiar smells, pungent and delicious.
My love, light the lamp of clear oil, so the Ancestors may gather and talk like
   parents
when their children are asleep.
Let us listen to the voices of our Ancients. Like us exiled,
they do not want to die and have the river of their seed disappear into desert
   sands.
Let me listen, in the fading smoke, as their welcome spirits visit.
My head on your breast warm as manioc steaming from the fire,
let me breathe the scent of our Dead, remember and be their living voice,
learn from them to live—
before I descend, like a coral diver,
to the soaring depths of sleep.

COWS IN THE SHADE

(1770)

Circling and circling the lazy meadow glare
the red tail sees exactly the right chance,
and life feeds life. Good afternoon, ladies,
how do you do? With your permission. Look:
Just up there, on that sunny vacant spot
a Pequot village died out, of the pox.
There must be more than sixty unmarked graves
up toward the tree line. Dug a few myself.

Surely they must have thought God died. Like me,
when I was pushed onboard, my life to feed
the coffers of a stranger. Yet things fall
together again. The truth is, the earth heals
over our fates as over a taken squirrel's.
Perhaps we are not the center. Perhaps you
young ladies are Creation's best success,
chewing the cud and contemplating time
with blank-eyed innocence. Just visited
a man I shall buy and set to work for me.
I can make up my investment in six months,
even if I give him forty percent.
I'll hire him out at haying first. Good day.
Let's see: If I can talk his master down . . .

SAP RISING

(1773)

As soon as the peepers start their nightly song,
I set my nets across the swollen creek,
ready for the alewives' headlong run upstream.
For two weeks I'll sell herring by the wagonload,
and I'll salt a barrel away for future need.
If the run is good this year, I'll buy my wife
before she shows, and get a bonus child.
Hauling nets in, I notice again how birds
conduct conversations with others of their kind.
That grand old man in his black-and-white-checked coat
and jolly red cap must be making a speech
in woodpeckerish. Just listen to him tap!
What are they saying, Brother Woodpecker's drums?

> *(Tenderest tidings, potential future mate:*
> *I lack! Seek poke, titillation. Trust luck.*

> . . .

> *(Triplequick chick will trade tricky tickles!)*

Hmmm. Must be a she-pecker tapping her answer back.
Some hollow tree trunk is about to become a home.
Another good haul, and this child will be born free.

FARM GARDEN

(ca. 1790)

By the time I was thirty-six I had been sold
three times. I had spun money out of sweat.
I'd been cheated and beaten. I had paid an enormous sum
for my freedom. And ten years farther on I've come
out here to my garden at the first faint hint of light
to inventory the riches I now hold.

My potatoes look fine, and my corn, my squash, my beans.
My tobacco is strutting, spreading its velvety wings.
My cabbages are almost as big as my head.
From labor and luck I have much profited.
I wish I could remember those praise-songs
we used to dance to, with the sacred drums.

My rooster is calling my hens from my stone wall.
In my meadow, my horses and my cows look up,
then graze again. My orchard boasts green fruit.
Yes, everything I own is dearly bought,
but gratitude is a never-emptying cup,
my life equal measures pain and windfall.

My effigies to scare raccoons and crows
frown fiercely, wearing a clattering fringe of shells,
like dancers in the *whatdidwecallit?* dance.
My wife and two of my children stir in my house.
For one thirty years enslaved, I have done well.
I am free and clear; not one penny do I owe.

I own myself—a five-hundred-dollar man—
and two thousand dollars' worth of family.
Of canoes and boats, right now I own twenty-nine.
Seventy acres of bountiful land is mine.
God, or gods, thanks for raining these blessings on me.
I turn around slowly. I own everything I scan.

THE FREEDOM BUSINESS

(ca. 1790)

Freeing people is good business, in principle.
You'd think they'd thank you for sixty percent
of their earnings while they repay your capital
investment: business and benevolence,
for once, going hand in hand. But people think
your freeing them means they are free to leave
or lollygag. And your money, carefully banked,
then paid to The Man out of brotherly love,
might as well be tossed down the privy hole.

The first person I freed cost sixty pounds,
and had repaid twenty when the fellow stole
away by night. The second turned around
and went back to his master, so I lost
four hundred dollars for nothing. And the third
and I simply decided it was best
to part company. Frankly, the reward
for freeing people is a broken heart.

My son Solomon (seventy-five pounds)
sent on a whaler, his young life cut short
by scurvy. My daughter (forty-four pounds)
marrying a fool and contracting a fatal disease.
I paid for a physician (forty pounds),
but Hannah died. God has mysterious ways.
And freedom is definitely not a matter of funds.
Freedom's a matter of making history,
of venturing forth toward a time when freedom is free.

From *Fortune's Bones: The Manumission Requiem*

In 1798, a slave named Fortune died at about the age of sixty. His owner, Dr. Preserved Porter, rendered the bones of his former slave so he could use the skeleton as a teaching tool. Fortune's bones now reside in the Mattatuck Museum in Waterbury, Connecticut.

ON ABRIGADOR HILL

(Dr. Preserved Porter)

For fifty years my feeling hands
have practiced the bone-setter's healing touch,
a gift inherited by Porter men.
I have manipulated joints,
cracked necks, and set my neighbors back to work.
I've bled and purged fever and flux,
inoculated for smallpox,
prescribed fresh air and vegetables,
cod-liver oil and laudanum,
and closed the lightless eyes of the new dead.

And I've been humbled by ignorance,
humbled by ignorance.

Herewith begins my dissection of
the former body of my former slave,
which served him who served me throughout his life,
and now serves the advance of science.
Note well how death softens the human skin,
making it almost transparent,
so that under my reverent knife—
the first cut takes my breath away,
it feels like cutting the whole world—
it falls open like bridal gossamer.

And I've been humbled by ignorance,
humbled by ignorance.

Standing on a new continent
beyond the boundaries of nakedness,
I am forever changed by what I see:
the complex, delicate organs
fitted perfectly in their shelter of bones,
the striated and smooth muscles,
the beautiful integuments,
the genius-strokes of thumb and knee.
In profound and awful intimacy,
I enter Fortune, and he enters me.

And I've been humbled by ignorance,
humbled by ignorance.

DINAH'S LAMENT

(Fortune's wife)

Miss Lydia doesn't clean the Doctor room.
She say she can't go in that room: she scared.
She make me take the dust-rag and the broom
and clean around my husband, hanging there.

Since she seen Fortune head in that big pot
Miss Lydia say that room make her feel ill,
sick with the thought of boiling human broth.
I wonder how she think it make me feel?

To dust the hands what use to stroke my breast;
to dust the arms what hold me when I cried;
to dust where his soft lips were, and his chest
what curved its warm against my back at night.

Through every season, sun-up to star light,
I heft, scrub, knead: one black woman alone,
except for my children. The world so white,
nobody know my pain, but Fortune bones.

NOT MY BONES

(Fortune)

I was not this body,
I was not these bones.
This skeleton was just my
temporary home.
Elementary molecules converged for a breath,
then danced on beyond my individual death.
And I am not my body,
I am not my body.

We are brief incarnations,
we are clouds in clothes.
We are water respirators,
we are how Earth knows.
I bore light passed on from an original flame;
while it was in my hands it was called by my name.
But I am not my body,
I am not my body.

You can own a man's body,
but you can't own his mind.
That's like making a bridle
to ride on the wind.
I will tell you one thing, and I'll tell you true:
Life's the best thing that can happen to you.
But you are not your body,
you are not your body.

You can own someone's body,
but the soul runs free.
It roams the night sky's
mute geometry.
You can murder hope, you can pound faith flat,
but, like weeds and wildflowers, they grow right back.
For you are not your body,
you are not your body.

24

You are not your body,
you are not your bones.
What's essential about you
is what can't be owned.
What's essential in you is your longing to raise
your itty-bitty voice in the cosmic praise.
For you are not your body,
you are not your body.

Well, I woke up this morning just so glad to be free,
glad to be free, glad to be free.
I woke up this morning in restful peace.
For I am not my body,
I am not my bones.
I am not my body,
glory hallelujah,
I am not my bones.
I am not my bones.   hopeful → goes on past body

From *Seneca Village*

The imagined lives of men, women, and children who lived in Manhattan's first significant community of African American property owners. Seneca Village existed from 1825–1857 and was razed for the creation of Central Park.

SKY-LAND

(Sara Matilda White, 1831)

Miz Elizabeth, that bump looks good on you!
Don't blush, Honey. Love is a joy to share.
Now, what are we doing today with that mop of hair?
Sit on down. I'll fetch warm water and shampoo.

This week: shagbark nut oil with peppermint.
Mortar and Pestle and I are on a quest
to find which combinations work the best,
kettle by kettle of crushed oil and scent.

You heard about Jane Bolden? Such a shame.
Lean back. But she was lustful to the end!
Acted like every man was her boyfriend.
Sometimes I was tempted to call her out of her name.

Pat dry, while I heat the oil. You heard about
that Nat Turner, that led slaves to rebel?
For two days whites in Virginia lived in hell
on earth like us, I hear. Yes, just: no doubt.

If justice means turning the tables around,
showing the cruel no mercy. That makes sense
by the natural logic of experience,
but it ain't the teaching my mama passed down.

Alright, Miz Elizabeth: cornrows again?
You're too tender-headed, Girl. Try not to flinch!
Fifty-five they killed, for which hundreds were lynched.
Yes, he was a hero; a man among men.

26

Nat Turner

He was hanged, flayed and quartered; they cut off his head.
Maybe God spoke to him. Maybe madness played a part.
But I believe vengeance harms the avenging heart.
Was he right or wrong? Ask the future. Ask the dead.

All done! Tell Obadiah to watch his back . . .
Thanks! Have a nice day! Yes, that's on my list
of things to ask, when I'm called to my rest
in that sky-land where everybody's black!

In November 1831, enslaved visionary Nat Turner led a well-planned, violent slave revolt in Virginia.

---

1. Where does this take place?
   - Their salon (North)
2. What are they talking about?

3. What is the major message of this poem
   - equality

- Virginia (Seneca Village)

- Nat Turner, Jane Bolden
   - rebellions

- political

- Fiction vs Fact

, Mistreatment
- inequality
- future of Blacks.

CONDUCTOR

(Nancy Morris, widow, ca. 1838)

When did my knees learn how to forecast rain,
and my hairbrush start yielding silver curls?
Of late, a short walk makes me short of breath,
and every day begins and ends with pain.
Just yesterday I was raising my girls;
now I'm alone, and making friends with death.

So let the railroad stop at my back door
for a hot meal. What do I have to lose?
The Lord has counted the hairs on my head
and made a little space under my floor.
All I ask of life is to be of use.
There'll be time to be careful when I'm dead.

Birth is a one-way ticket to the grave:
I've learned that much slowly, over the years,
watching my body age. Time is a thief,
and what we give away is all we can save.
So bring on the runaways! I know no fear.
Let life have meaning, if it must be brief.

[handwritten: negative / positive]

The Underground Railroad, a secret network of routes leading from the South to free-
dom in Canada, operated from ca. 1501–1865. People who risked their lives to help slaves
escape on this route were called "conductors."

[handwritten: Only way to save something is to give it away]

THE COTILLION

(Angelina Morris, 1844)

Mama made my gown of Swiss muslin gauze
over satin, with matching satin trim,
tiny pleats at the waist, a rouleau hem,
and modest front and back décolletés.

Clothig

Long kidskin gloves. A shawl of Belgian lace.
In my embroidered bag, a Spanish fan.
My hot-combed hair at my nape in a bun,
curling-iron curls on each side of my face.

Tim hired a liveried carriage for the night.
He wore a tailcoat, brought me a corsage.
(We earn good money now, so we can splurge,
this once, pretending we're rich socialites.)

In petticoats, ribbons, and ostrich plumes,
with watch chains, snuff boxes, and monocles,
we were enchanted individuals
last night, Cinderellas without our brooms.

The ballroom looked elegant, and the band
played waltzes and quadrilles. Colored New York
danced in its finery, forgetting work,
insult, and slavery still in our land.

1844 was the beginning of a period of national financial prosperity.

ADDRESS

(Delivered by Mrs. Maria W. Stewart ca. 1845)

Do the sons of Africa have no souls?
Do they feel no ambition? No desires?
Can a slave not be noble? A master be a fool?

Shall the earth be inherited by the fierce?
Shall ignorance continue to enchain
the ignorant, so their ignorance grows worse?

Shall we always be judged the lesser men?
Are we not equally able to achieve?
Not statesmen, scientists, historians?

Have we no heroes, gallant, fearless, brave?
No lecturers on natural history?
Are the distinguished extinguished by being enslaved
in this nation of freedom and democracy?
Lord, Ethiopia stretches her hands to Thee!

Essayist, lecturer, abolitionist, and women's rights activist Maria Stewart (1803–1879) was the earliest known American woman to lecture in public on political themes and leave copies of her texts. Her first publication, a twelve-page pamphlet entitled "Religion and the Pure Principles of Morality" (1831), revealed her distinctive style, a mix of political analysis and religious exhortation. Her message, highly controversial coming from the pen of a woman, called upon African Americans to organize against slavery in the South and to resist racist restrictions in the North. She invoked both the Bible and the Constitution of the United States as documents proclaiming a universal birthright to freedom and justice.

THOMPSON AND SEAMAN VOWS, AFRICAN UNION CHURCH

(ca. 1847)

Miss Charlotte Thompson, daughter of Ada
Thompson of Seneca and the late John,
and Timothy James Seaman, son
of the late Nancy Seaman, on Sunday.
Reverend Rush performed the ceremony.
The bride (twenty-four) was educated
by a literate friend, and by seeing
the African Theatre Company's
productions of *Macbeth* and *Richard III*.
She teaches in Colored School #3.
Her father was a slave. Her mother, freed
by a clause in her late mistress's will,
sews and sells exquisite lace lingerie.
The bridegroom (twenty-six) cannot read or write,
but ciphers and is a skilled carpenter.
His mother was slaved to an early death.
She told him he was descended from kings.

WORDS AND WHISPERS

(Address delivered by Frederick Douglass ca. 1848)

A battle won is easily described;
the moral growth of a great nation requires
description and reflection, to be seen.
Hey, that's MINE!

A little learning is a dangerous thing;
the want of learning a calamity.

You better give it back!

The life of a nation can be secure
only while it is virtuous and true.

I MEAN it!

America has been false to the past,
false to the present, and solemnly binds
herself to be false to the future, too.

Give it back!

No harvest without plowing up the ground;
no rain without a rumble of dark clouds.

Oh, yeah?

It is easier to build strong children
than to piece back together broken men.

He started it!!

For he who sows the wind reaps the whirlwind.

Yessum.

Born a slave in Maryland, Frederick Douglass (1803–1870) is one of the most prominent figures in African American and U.S. history. He was a firm believer in the equality of all people.

LITTLE BOX

"A female still born child of Egbert Stairs (colored) & Catherine Cochran
his wife (white) was buried in All Angels' churchyard, November 18, 1849"

Someone has died, who will never see the black
joylight expand in her mother's blue eyes.
Who will never grasp a pinky, nor be danced
up, down, and around and lullabied all night.
Someone who will never come to realize
that her Dada's palms aren't dirty, they're just brown.
Who made HER mother, HIM father, then broke their hearts.
Who is their shooting star, glimpsed only once.
Someone who will never laugh, or play, or care . . .

Praying that little box into the earth,
Rev. Peters asks forgiveness for his faint faith.
He thinks of the life of pain Someone was spared.

light

, what does symbol mean

MIRACLE IN THE COLLECTION PLATE

(Rev. Christopher Rush, 1850)

Brothers and sisters, we know why we're here
this evening. The sad news has traveled fast
of Brother James's capture. For three years
he lived amongst us, tasting happiness.

His wife and child are here with us tonight.
God bless you, Sister. Without a goodbye,
James was handcuffed, and shoved on a steamboat
to Baltimore, to be sold—legally!

Neighbors, we know that upright, decent man:
James Hamlet—a loving husband, father, friend.
Many of us would gladly risk the fine
or prison sentence, if we could help him.

My friends, all is not lost! It's not too late!
We are told that Brother James may be redeemed!
His buyer will sell him! But we cannot wait:
we need eight hundred dollars to free him.

Eight hundred. I know every penny counts,
living from widow's mite to widow's mite.
But with God's help, we can raise that enormous amount!
Let's make a miracle in the collection plate!

In 1850 the U.S. Congress passed the Fugitive Slave Law, which made any Federal
marshal or other official who did not arrest an alleged runaway slave liable to a fine of
$1,000. Law enforcement officials everywhere now had a duty to arrest anyone sus-
pected of being a runaway slave on no more evidence than a claimant's sworn testimony
of ownership. The suspected slave could not ask for a jury trial or testify on his or her
own behalf. In addition, any person aiding a runaway slave by providing food or shelter
was subject to six months' imprisonment and a $1,000 fine. Officers who captured a fu-
gitive slave were entitled to a bonus for their work. Slave owners only needed to supply
an affidavit to a Federal marshal to capture an escaped slave. Since any suspected slave

was not eligible for a trial, this led to many free blacks being conscripted into slavery, as they had no rights in court and could not defend themselves against accusations. James Hamlet was the first fugitive arrested under the new law. His African American and abolitionist friends raised the money necessary to purchase his freedom.

SISTERS OF CHARITY

(Sarah Matilda White, 1853)

More Irish seem to arrive here every day,
like rats fleeing a ship that's going down.
Their women troll our streets for men at night;
their children run wild all day in shantytown.

They come in coffin ships, with little more
than faith and hunger. Ignorant, unskilled,
they seem hell-bent on making themselves less,
like prodigal sons content to live in swill.

People who have nothing will rob the poor
to feed their children. Now I lock the house
and clutch my purse, as fearful as the rich.
They're starved of hope, desperate, and unwashed.

But I do like that flock of Irish nuns
who swoop like crows, catching truants by the ear
and marching them to school, then wake the tarts
to steer them toward respectable careers.

They are taking thousands of white fugitive slaves
who can't imagine better lives beyond
full stomachs, work, and a hovel called home,
and teaching them to dream of a free dawn!

The Irish famine refugees met with vehement racism when they arrived in America.
Many newspaper articles and cartoons depicted them as inferior to blacks. Father John
Hughes (1797–1864), a fierce advocate of abolition and the rights of Irish immigrants,
was the first Roman Catholic bishop, and then archbishop, of New York. He fought
strenuously on behalf of the Irish, forcing reforms in the anti-Catholic public schools,
inviting Roman Catholic religious orders to come to the city, and instituting a system of
parochial schools (including four universities) that taught reading, writing, arithmetic,
and personal responsibility.

UNCLE EPIPHANY

(ca. 1855)

Our African Ancestors always knew
a change was in the making: even then,
when each day was a cloudbank they flew through,
solid grey to the encircling horizon.
Had they not known how lucky we would be,
how could they go on? They trusted the sun
of life's infinite possibility,
which they could not see, though they knew it shone.

Epiphanies appear, from time to time,
when I see through the cloud. This secret gift
ignites my eyes, and makes me smile and hum,
as one who knows that time and we are mist
hiding Light's ever-changing panorama,
where the future holds a President Obama.

From *Miss Crandall's School for Young Ladies & Little Misses of Color*

In 1831, twenty-eight-year-old Prudence Crandall of Canterbury, Connecticut, opened a boarding school for young women. In 1832, Crandall began admitting young African American women as students. The townspeople responded by poisoning the school's water, setting fire to the schoolhouse, and putting Crandall on trial. The school was forced to close in September 1834.

THE BOOK

Jolted insensible mile upon mile,
a thin, high-breasted, sloe-eyed yellow girl.
Deferential but wearing the latest style
of Paris bonnet from which one brown curl
has broken free and frolics below her jaw,
all the stagecoach ride from Philadelphia
she has followed the beckoning finger of destiny
toward the place where she'll shoulder the burden of being free:
I shall learn, I shall teach. The book in her small gloved hands
hasn't seemed a Bible to the inquisitive eyes
of her fellow travelers. Almost memorized,
it comforts her as she watches the changing lands,
a friend to travel with into this chance
to bridge for her people the abyss of ignorance.

FAMILY

My master/father sent me up from South
Carolina to Boston as a nine-year-old.
My mother's illiterate silence has been a death.
I wonder if she still labors in his fields.
His sister, dutiful but cold as snow,
gave me a little room in her house, below
the stairs with the Irish servants, who hated me
for the fatal flaw in my genealogy.
For the first time in my life I am at home
in this bevy of scholars, my first family.
Here, the wallpapers welcome me into every room,
and the mirrors see me, not my pedigree.
My sisters, Jerusha, Emilia, Elizabeth . . .
But Mama's unlettered silence is a death.

THE TAO OF THE TRIAL

Miss Crandall, you stand accused of knowingly
teaching colored persons not resident of the state
without prior consent. What is your plea?

The Teacher does not instruct. The Teacher waits.

Girl, has anyone been teaching anything to you and your friends?

Who taught you how to plead the Fifth Amendment?

Your Honor, I submit as evidence
of the alleged teaching of alleged students
this colored girl here, who openly reads books
and gazes skyward, who has been overheard
conversing animatedly in polysyllabic words
and referring off-handedly to the ancient Greeks.

The Teacher teaches, without words and without action,
simplicity, patience, and compassion.

MISS ANN ELIZA HAMMOND

I brought here, in a bag between my breasts,
money from Mama's friend who had bought herself,
then saved enough, by working without rest,
to free four friends. This woman gave me her wealth
of carefully folded dollars so I could take
Miss Crandall's course of study. And within a week
of my arrival, I was summoned to appear in court.
The judge ruled I'd have to pay a fine, depart,
or be whipped naked.
                        Honey, the first white fool
that thinks he gone whip me better think again.
Touch me, and you'll draw back a nub, white man.
I ain't payin', and I'm stayin'. People's dreams brought me to this school.
I'm their future, in a magic looking glass.
That judge and the councilmen can kiss my rusty black.

ETYMOLOGY

The filth hissed at us when we venture out—
always in twos or threes, never alone—
seems less a language *spoken* than one *spat*
in savage plosives, primitive, obscene:
a cavemob *nya-nya,* limited in frame
of reference and novelty, the same
suggestions of what we or they could do
or should, *ad infinitum.* Yesterday
a mill girl spat a phrase I'd never heard
before. I stopped and looked at her, perplexed.
I derived its general meaning from the context
but was stumped by the etymology of one word.
What was its source? Which demon should we thank
for words it must be an abomination to think?

ALBERT HINKLEY

Last Sunday, a white boy openly smiled at me
where I sat with my sisters at the back of the Baptist church.
When the pastor spoke of the sin of slavery,
the white boy looked back with his eyebrows arched.
I could read his thoughts, but I dared not meet his glance,
for nothing must pass between us, not one chance
for gossip to pounce with glee on one shared smile.
No one must think of us as eligible girls.

Waylaid by ruffians as we reached the ford,
our wagon was overturned. Our sodden skirts
weighted and slowed us, but no one was hurt.
Splashing to me, his eyes looking truly scared,
that boy took my hand. *"Let me help you, Miss.*
From this day forward, I am an Abolitionist."

WORTH

For Ruben Ahoueya

Today in America people were bought and sold:
five hundred for a "likely Negro wench."
If someone at auction is worth her weight in gold,
how much would she be worth by pound? By ounce?
If I owned an unimaginable quantity of wealth,
could I buy an iota of myself?
How would I know which part belonged to me?
If I owned part, could I set my part free?
It must be worth something—maybe a lot—
that my great-grandfather, they say, killed a lion.
They say he was black, with muscles as hard as iron,
that he wore a necklace of the claws of the lion he'd fought.
How much do I hear, for his majesty in my blood?
I auction myself. And I make the highest bid.

From *Carver: A Life in Poems*

A portrait in poems of the life of George Washington Carver, botanist, inventor, painter, musician, and teacher.

WATKINS LAUNDRY AND APOTHECARY

Imagine a child at your door,
offering to do your wash,
clean your house, cook,
to weed your kitchen garden
or paint you a bunch of flowers
in exchange for a meal.
A spindly ten-year-old, alone
and a stranger in town, here to go
to our school for colored children.
His high peep brought tears:
sleeping in a barn and all that,
nary mama nor kin,
but only white folks
he left with their blessing,
his earthly belongings
in a handkerchief tied to a stick.

I've brought a houseful of children
into this world, concentrating on
that needle's eye into eternity.
But ain't none of them children mine.
Well, of course I moved him on in.
He helped me with my washings,
brought me roots from the woods
that bleached them white folks' sheets
brighter than sunshine. He could fill
a canning jar with leaves and petals
so when you lifted the lid,
a fine perfume flooded your senses.
White bodices and pantalettes danced
around George on my line.

He was sweet with the neighbor children.
Taught the girls to crochet.
Showed the boys
a seed he said held a worm
cupped hands warmed so it wriggled and set
the seed to twitching.
Gave them skills and wonders.
Knelt with me at bedtime.

He was the child the good Lord gave
and took away before I got more
than the twinkle of a glimpse
at the man he was going to be.
It happened one Saturday afternoon.
George was holding a black-eyed Susan,
talking about how the seed
that this flower grew from
carried a message from a flower
that bloomed a million years ago,
and how this flower
would send the message on
to a flower that was going to bloom
in a million more years.
Praise Jesus, I'll never forget it.

He left to find a teacher that knew
more than he knew.
I give him my Bible.
I keep his letters
in the bureau, tied with a bow.
He always sends a dried flower.

1877—With the blessing of his foster parents, Moses and Susan Carver, George moves
to Neosho, Missouri, about eight miles from his home in Diamond Grove, to attend the
closest school for Negro children. This begins his long search for an education.

OLD SETTLERS' REUNION

When I filed my claim back in April eighty-six,
this country weren't nothing but prairie grass,
rippling pink, blue, and yellow flowers
as far as the eye could squint.
Six years I cut tough turf from dawn
to way past suppertime, and drove my team back
to the sod house and barn
my first bride and I built together
like children playing with blocks.
Three of my children were born there.
I had two hundred acres, mostly in wheat.
To my north was Bothwick, to my south, Barnd.
To my east,
well, there's a story to tell.
Every other homesteader for counties around,
had at least a wife, and most had families.
And all of us were white
except for the colored boy, George.
I think his name was Carver.

He kept to himself, pretty much,
but was always sort of joyous when you met, and humble,
like he'd just been told
the most marvelous, flattering joke.
He took in wash when he was more
hard up than usual, and played the accordion
so your feet didn't know where
your backside was going.

We never talked much. He lasted a couple of years,
then Lennon bought his hundred and sixty acres.
Sometimes, in the half-light of a winter's morning, I heard
George's clear tenor like a church bell over the snow.

1886—Carver homesteads on the "sod house frontier" in Ness County, Kansas.

FOUR A.M. IN THE WOODS

Darkness softens, a thin
tissue of mist between trees.
One by one the day's
uncountable voices come out
like twilight fireflies, like stars.
The perceiving self sits
with his back against rough bark,
casting ten thousand questions into the future.
As shadows take shape, the curtains part
for the length of time it takes to gasp,
and behold, the purpose of his
life dawns on him.

CAFETERIA FOOD

Even when you've been living on
wild mushrooms, hickory nuts,
occasional banquet leftovers sneaked
out of the hotel kitchen by a colored cook,
and weeds; even when you know it feeds you
mind and body, keeps you going
through the gauntlet
of whispered assault
as you wait in line;
even when it's free
except for the pride
you have to pay by eating
alone in the basement;
even when there's a lot of it,
hot meat or chicken and potatoes
and fresh baked bread and buttery
vegetables; even when there's dessert;
even when you can count on it day after day;
even when it's good,
it's bad.

1891—Carver transfers to Iowa State Agricultural College, Ames, Iowa, believing that in
this way he can better serve the Negro people.

CALLED

Washington yammers on about his buckets.
Under the poorly pruned catalpa trees
the children of slaves slave on in ignorance.
For what but service is a man thus gifted?
(The set jaw, the toward-distance-looking eyes:
from the fly in the buttermilk, the butterfly in the cave.)
. . . your salary, duties, the school of agriculture
you will establish, your office key . . . A flash
twenty years ahead: this mecca,
this garden. *Good Christ, a whole Africa*
to save, right under my nose.

1896—Carver gets his MA degree and accepts Booker T. Washington's invitation to join the faculty of Tuskegee Institute. There he starts a new department and becomes the first Negro director of a U.S.D.A. Agricultural Experiment Station.

MY PEOPLE

Strutting around here acting all humble,
when everybody knows
he's the only one here
got a master's degree
from a white man's college.
Everybody knows his salary
is double ours. He's got two singles
in Rockefeller Hall; the rest of us
bachelors share doubles. The extra room
is for his "collections."
A pile of you-know-what,
if you ask me.
All that fake politeness, that white accent.
He thinks he's better than us.
Wears those mis-matched suits every day, too:
white men's castoffs with the sleeves too short,
the trousers all bagged out at the knees.
His ties look like something
he made himself.
Always some old weed in his lapel,
like he's trying to be dapper.
It makes you want to laugh.
Talking all those big words,
quoting poems at you
in that womanish voice.
So high and mighty,
he must think he's white.
Wandering around through the fields
like a fool, holding classes in the dump.
Always on his high horse, as if his
wasn't the blackest face on the faculty,
as if he wasn't a nigger.

CHEMISTRY 101

A canvas apron over his street clothes,
Carver leads his chemistry class into
the college dump. The students follow, a claque
of ducklings hatched by hens. Where he
sees a retort, a Bunsen burner,
a mortar, zinc sulfate, they see
a broken bowl, a broken lantern,
a rusty old flatiron, a fruit jar top.
Their tangle of twine, his lace.
He turns, a six-inch length of copper tubing
in one hand. "Now, what can we do with this?"
Two by two, little lights go on.
One by hesitant one, dark hands are raised.
The waters of imagining, their element.

FROM AN ALABAMA FARMER

Dere Dr. Carver, l bin folloring
the things l herd you say last planting time.
l give my cow more corn, less cottonseed
and my creme chirns mo better butter. I'm
riting to you today, Sir, jes to tell
you at l furtulize: 800 pounds
to the acur las March. Come harves, well
it were a bompercrop. How did you found
out you coud use swamp mock? l presheate
your anser Dr. Carver by mail soon.
What maid my cotton grow? It do fele grate
to see the swet off your brow com to bloom.
l want to now what maid my miricle.
Your humbel servint (name illegible)

BEDSIE READING

For St. Mark's Episcopal, Good Friday 1999

In his careful welter of dried leaves and seeds,
soil samples, quartz pebbles, notes-to-myself, letters,
on Dr. Carver's bedside table
next to his pocket watch,
folded in Aunt Mariah's Bible:
The Bill of Sale.
Seven hundred dollars
for a thirteen-year-old girl named Mary.

He moves it from passage
to favorite passage.
Fifteen cents
for every day she had lived.
Three hundred and fifty dollars
for each son.
No charge
for two stillborn daughters
buried out there with the Carvers' child.

This new incandescent light makes
his evening's reading unwaveringly easy,
if he remembers to wipe his spectacles.
He turns to the blossoming story
of Abraham's dumbstruck luck,
of Isaac's pure trust in his father's wisdom.
Seven hundred dollars for all of her future.
He shakes his head.

> When the ram bleats from the thicket,
>   Isaac . . .   like me . . .   understands
> the only things you can ever
>   really . . .   trust . . .
> are . . .
>   the natural order . . .

>   . . . and the Creator's love . . .
>   spiraling . . .
>   out of chaos . . .

Dr. Carver smoothes the page
and closes the book
on his only link with his mother.

He folds the wings of his spectacles
and bows his head for a minute.
Placing the Bible on the table
he forgets again at first, and blows at the light, _candle?_
Then he lies back dreaming as the bulb cools. _Right?_

POULTRY HUSBANDRY

(Tuskegee, 1902)

Raising chickens is a
dawn-to-dawn,
no-Sabbath proposition.
Carver is a botanist.
Yet, bowing before Mr. Washington's mandate,
Carver is named Superintendent of Poultry Operations,
in addition to teaching seven classes,
testing seed, examining soils, running
the Agricultural Experiment Station,
preparing bulletins,
overseeing the dairy's one hundred four cows,
and maintaining a laboratory,
with the assistance of the two or three
work-study students the budget allows.

Washington requires daily
Poultry Yard Reports,
writes from Ithaca
that it doesn't make much sense
to have twenty-seven roosters
for forty-nine hens.
He writes from Syracuse
that there should be twice as many
chicks, given the number of eggs set
and incubated. He writes from Boston
to suggest chicks be purchased.
He telegraphs from New York City
to point out that thirty-nine eggs
are unaccounted for.

Carver answers, "I have faith in the chickens."
But he watches twenty roosters
weed themselves down to ten.
He sees a pecking order established
by ruthless omnivores, by cannibals.

He sees chickens kill each other
out of sheer boredom. He learns
that if you don't stop them,
chickens will peck their pariahs
to ribs and drumsticks.

Slowly, he learns a new vocabulary.
Blackhead: general weakness, unthriftiness,
sulphur-colored droppings. Mortality high.
Sorehead: wart-like nodules covered by black scabs
on bare parts of the head, the feet, and around
the vent. Mortality high.
Coccidiosis: unthriftiness, diarrhea. Mortality high.
Epidemic Tremor: loss of balance,
wobbling gait, prostration, kicking.
Mortality high.
Cholera. Mortality high.
Bronchitis. Mortality high.
Newcastle. Can wipe out
your whole flock.

Toward the end
of one of his daily pre-dawn rambles,
Carver stops at the poultry yard.
He notes the unlocked latch, the gate ajar.
Old Teddy Roosevelt gives the man a beady look,
flaps his wings, stretches
his scrawny, good-for-nothing neck,
and again, hope bleaches the horizon.

1905

Looking out of the picture, a wild-haired,
gentle-eyed young German man stands
before a blackboard of incomprehensible equations.
Meanwhile, back in the quotidian,
Carver takes the school to the poor.

He outfits an open truck
with shelves for his jars
of canned fruit and compost,
bins for his croker sacks of seeds.
He travels roads barely discernible
on the county map,
teaching former field-slaves
how to weave ditch weeds
into pretty table place mats,
how to keep their sweet potatoes from rotting
before winter hunger sets in,
how to make preacher-pleasing
mock fried chicken
without slaughtering a laying hen.
He notes patches of wild chicory
the farmers could collect
to free themselves from their taste
for high-priced imported caffeine.

He and his student assistants bump along
shoulder to shoulder in the high cab,
a braided scale of laughter
trailing above their raised dust.
Today, Carver is explaining,
as far as he understands it,
that fellow Einstein's "Special Theory of Relativity."
He's hardly gotten to Newtonian Space
when a platoon of skinny dogs
announces the next farm.

As they pull up,
a black man and his boy straighten,
two rows of shin-high cotton apart.
With identical gestures they remove
straw hats, wipe their foreheads with their sleeves.
Their welcoming glance meets Carver's eyes
at the velocity of light.

1905—Carver initiates the Jesup wagon, outfitting a horse-drawn wagon to take his agricultural teaching to the rural poor.

VEIL-RAISERS

Sometimes one light burned late
in The Oaks, the stately home of the great
Principal, Booker T. He sat and wrote
note after note, controlling faculty,
philanthropists, and family
with spiderweb reins.
When a plank broke and he plunged
into white hopelessness,
he shook himself
and rang up to the third floor,
where a student exchanging service
for tuition sproinged to his feet.

The breathless summons reached
Carver's cluttered rooms
down in Rockefeller Hall,
where he dozed in his easy chair.
He still had lab notes to write,
tomorrow's classes to prepare,
letters, and his Bible reading.
He'd been up, as always,
since that godliest hour
when light is created anew,
and he would wake again
in a few more hours.
Roused, he nodded,
exchanged slippers for brogans.

You saw them sometimes
if you were sneaking in past curfew,
after a tête-à-tête on a town girl's porch:
shoulder to shoulder
and dream to dream,
two veil-raisers.
Walking our people
into history.

HOW A DREAM DIES

It was 1915, the year
of trenches and poison gas,
when Booker T. Washington
rushed home from New Haven
to die in his own bed.
For the first days after the funeral
Carver sat and rocked, sat
and rocked. For months
he could not teach,
would not go into the lab.
He sat in his room, he rocked.
His duties were reduced
to supervising the study hall,
where he sat at the front of the room
staring into his hands.

In a vision the first time they met,
Carver had been shown a lifelong partnership.
He paced the campus. He rocked.
He had seen Washington and Carver together
winning back the birthright of the disinherited.
This is how a dream dies.
In the news Europe's tribal feuds
spread to the colonies,
a conflagration of madness.
As if fifty thousand shot and bayoneted men
strewn in an unplowed field
could make right any righter.
As if might
made wrong any less wrong.
All of the dead are of the same nation.

His presence turned laughter down
to whispers. "He acts like he's lost
his best friend." *Uh-uh: He acts
like he's lost his faith.*

1915—Booker T. Washington dies. The monument erected at Tuskegee in his honor depicts him lifting a veil from the eyes of a male slave who is rising from a kneeling position.

THE DIMENSIONS OF THE MILKY WAY

(Discovered by Harlow Shapley, 1918)

Behind the men's dorm
at dusk on a late May evening,
Carver lowers the paper
and watches the light change.
He tries to see Earth
across a distance
of twenty-five thousand light-years,
from the center of the Milky Way:
a grain of pollen, a spore
of galactic dust.
He looks around:
that shagbark, those swallows,
the fireflies, that blasted mosquito;
this beautiful world.
A hundred billion stars
in a roughly spherical flattened disc
with a radius of one hundred light-years.
Imagine that.
He catches a falling star.
Well, Lord, this
infinitesimal speck
could fill the universe with praise.

RUELLIA NOCTIFLORA

A colored man come running at me out of the woods
last Sunday morning.
The junior choir was going to be singing
at Primitive Baptist over in Notasulga,
and we were meeting early to practice.
I remember wishing I was barefoot
in the heavy, cool-looking dew.
And suddenly this tall, rawbone wild man
come puffing out of the woods, shouting
Come see! Come see!
Seemed like my mary janes just stuck
to the gravel. Girl, my heart
like to abandon ship!

Then I saw by the long tin cylinder
slung over his shoulder on a leather strap,
and his hoboish tweed jacket
and the flower in his lapel
that it was the Professor.
He said, gesturing,
his tan eyes a blazing,
that last night,
walking in the full moon light,
he'd stumbled on
a very rare specimen:
Ruellia noctiflora,
the night-blooming wild petunia.
Said he suddenly sensed a fragrance
and a small white glistening.
It was clearly a petunia:
The yellow future beckoned
from the lip of each tubular flower,
a blaring star of frilly, tongue-like petals.
He'd never seen this species before.
As he tried to place it,
the flowers gaped wider,

65

catching the moonlight,
suffusing the night with its scent.
All night he watched it
promise silent ecstasy to moths.

If we hurried, I could see it
before it closed to contemplate
becoming seed.
Hand in hand, we entered
the light-spattered morning-dark woods.
Where he pointed was only a white flower
until I saw him seeing it.

GOLIATH

for J. B.

Another lynching. Madness grips the South.
A black man's hacked-off penis in his mouth,
his broken body torched. The terrorized
blacks cower, and the whites are satanized.
His students ask, in Carver's Bible class:
Where is God now? What does He want from us?

Professor Carver smiles. "God is right here.
Don't lose contact with Him. Don't yield to fear.
Fear is the root of hate, and hate destroys
the hater. When Saul's army went to war
against the Philistines, the Israelites
lost contact, fearful of Goliath's might.

"When we lose contact, we see only hate,
only injustice, a giant so great
its shadow blocks our sun. But David slew
Goliath with the only things he knew:
the slingshot of intelligence, and one
pebble of truth. And the battle was done.

"We kill Goliath by going about
the business of the universal good
which our Creator wills, obediently
yielding to Him the opportunity
to work wonders through us for all of His children.
That's all. Read 1 Samuel 17:47."

HOUSE WAYS AND MEANS

The Chair cedes Mr. Carver ten minutes.

Mr. Chairman, the United Peanut Growers
Association wants me to tell you
about the peanut's possibilities.
I come from Tuskegee, Alabama.
I am engaged in agricultural
research. I've given some attention to
the peanut, and I plan to give much more.
I'm greatly interested in southern crops,
their possibilities. The peanut is
one of the most remarkable I know.
If I may have some space to put things down,
I'd like to show them to you . . .
. . . chocolate-covered peanuts . . . peanut milk . . .
. . . a breakfast food. I'm sorry that you can't
taste this, so I will taste it for you. Mmmm.

John Tilson (R-Connecticut): Do you
want a watermelon to go with that?

Well, if you want dessert, that comes in well,
but we can get along without dessert.
The recent war has taught us that. Now, these
are dyes that can be made from peanut skins.
This is a quinine substitute. A food
for diabetics, low in starch and sugar . . .

1921—Carver appears before the U.S. House of Representatives, Committee on Ways
and Means, in support of a protective tariff on peanuts.

"GOD'S LITTLE WORKSHOP"

A hand-lettered sign above
the room number on the closed door.
"Do Not Disturb"
written in the air.
The Professor had had another vision
of an experiment he should try,
a question he should ask.
The Creator's small, still voice
asked *What would happen*
if you made a resin of peanut oil,
and added a little bit
of this nitric acid here,
some of that sulphuric acid there,
some alcohol, some camphor,
a little of this, a little of that?
Would the molecules form clusters
tightly bonded into one plastic
which could be shaped and molded?

A thin, white silence issued
from the door seams,
settled on all who knew
the door was closed again,
made them walk softly,
modulate their laughter,
take themselves seriously.

The Creator asked
What about elasticity?
Is Ficus elastica *the only plant on earth*
whose sap is a latex?
What about Asclepias syriaca?
What about Ipomoea batatas?
Coagulated and stabilized, vulcanized
and compounded with an inert filler,

would their sap become a half-solid, half-liquid
which deforms under applied stress
yet after stretching recovers completely?

The Professor took his Eurekas on grueling
medicine-show lecture tours.
He spoke softly, holding up
his peanut axle grease,
his peanut diesel fuel,
his peanut gasoline,
his peanut insecticide,
his nitroglycerine,
his plastics,
his rubber,
his sleeping compound,
his iron tonic,
his goiter treatment,
his faith, his science,
his miracles.

EUREKA

(November 1924)

His first time in New York,
as one of several speakers
before a conference crowd,
the Professor is allotted twenty minutes.
He abbreviates his talk,
stops abruptly, adds:
I never have to grope for methods;
the method is revealed
the moment I am inspired
to create something new.

The *New York Times* ridicules him,
the school at which he is employed,
and the entire Negro race.
Proving its prophecy, it editorializes:
Talk of that sort simply will bring
ridicule on an admirable institution
and on the race for which it has done
and still is doing so much.
Because REAL scientists
do not ascribe their successes
to "inspiration."

MINERALOGY

For the staff of the Carver National Monument,
Diamond Grove, Missouri

The only thing he still wanted
that a millionaire could buy,
Ford's good friend answered,
was a big diamond.
In Ford's mind,
on Carver's long, skinny, wrinkled
anthracite finger,
a stone to dazzle an entire
classification system of eyes.

Ford told how he bought a flawless
many-carat stone, had it set
in a masculine ring,
and sent it off
gift-wrapped.
When next in Tuskegee
to visit Carver and throw
some money around,
Ford asked where the ring was.
Carver lovingly set aside
several dusty shoe boxes of specimens
and opened a box labeled MINERALS.

He showed Ford his phosphate pebble,
found in an Iowa creek bed,
his microcline feldspar, found
in the Alabama woods, his smoky quartz,
kicked up by his boot toe
in a Kansas wheat-field, his fluorite,
sent by a Kentucky spelunker, his
marcasite, sent by an English mineralogist
in exchange for a piece of information,
and here it was, his diamond, the gift
of his dear friend, Henry.

Carver held the ring up to the window.
Ford saw by its faceted luster
that Carver's eyes weren't black, they were brown—
no, they were sparklets of citrine light.

LAST TALK WITH JIM HARDWICK

(A "found" poem)

When I die I will live again.
By nature I am a conserver.
I have found Nature
to be a conserver, too.
Nothing is wasted
or permanently lost
in Nature. Things
change their form,
but they do not cease
to exist. After
I leave this world
I do not believe I am through.
God would be a bigger fool
than even a man
if He did not conserve
the human soul,
which seems to be
the most important thing
He has yet done in the universe.
When you get your grip
on the last rung of the ladder
and look over the wall
as I am now doing,
you don't need their proofs:
You see.
You know
you will not die.

MOTON FIELD

(January 1943)

From the airfield a few miles down the road
a new droning crowds out laughter from the lawn,
talk in the corridor, automobiles,
and the occasional crow.
There goes one—no, two, three, four:
Like lost geese they circle in practice runs
from sunup to dusk.

The Professor's palsied right hand
stutters answers to letters heaped beside his bed.
Behind them the amaryllis on the sill surrenders
to the cold sky its slow-motion skyrocket.
Beyond the clasped flame of its bud
a P-40 zooms in at five o'clock,
high as a Negro has ever been.

Such a shame, thinks the Professor.
Might-have-been ploughshares, hammered
into swords. Sighing, he signs his shaky name.
As Nelson tilts the stick to his left, pulls it
slightly toward him, pushes his left rudder pedal,
thumbs-up at the flight-instructor, grins,
and makes a sky-roaring victory-roll.

1941—The first "Tuskegee Airmen" recruited for an experimental U.S. Army program
arrive at Tuskegee.

1942—On December 9, the fighter pilots of the 99th Air Pursuit Squadron, the first
graduating class of the Tuskegee Airmen, receive their orders to join U.S. combat
forces in Europe. My father, Melvin M. Nelson, was in the class of 1943.

1943—On January 5, George Washington Carver dies in his sleep in his room in
Dorothy Hall.

From *Sweethearts of Rhythm*

The International Sweethearts of Rhythm was the first all-female interracial swing band. The women performed on the American home front during the 1940s, when the world was at war. In this sequence, the instruments tell their story.

BUGLE CALL RAG

(Nova Lee McGee on Trumpet)

No trumpet has ever been tempted
not to funambulate
on the filament of a melody.
We're all stars; we were made for the limelight.

I was bought second-hand in Biloxi.
(I'd been honorably discharged by the Army band.)
I moaned, seeing this as a step down;
to be played by a woman: I, who'd been played by a real man.

But the first time we stepped out front and center
and blasted the rafters with a long-held E,
I knew that all those years of playing marches
had kept me from being all I was meant to be.

CHATTANOOGA CHOO-CHOO

(Twin Ione or Irene Gresham on Tenor Sax)

Some days the earth seems to reverse its spin,
and everyone seems to be flailing around in the dark.
The day war was declared, one of the twins
unpacked me for practice as usual, and set to work.

She performed the daily ritual of the reed—
soaking the reed, trimming it, fitting it in,
tightening the ligature. She bowed her head,
then lifted me and eased me into song.

She was pushing herself through me to an open space
where people can be one.

It was "Chattanooga Choo-Choo," but it was a prayer for peace.
She was trying to change the world through sound.

JUMP, JUMP, JUMP

(Helen Saine on Alto Sax)

From ballroom to ballroom, the unsleeping eye of Jim Crow
ever upon us, we traveled the United States
of colored America, bouncing on backcountry roads
and gliding on highways. At picnics, we practiced our charts,
our polished brass gleaming. We welcomed farm children who ran
one or two miles to be able to listen and dance.

> *Do you want to jump, children?*
> *—Yeah!*
> *Do you want to jump, children?*
> *—Yeah!*

Domestics, farm laborers, new hires in factory jobs;
the Apollo, the Royal, the Regal, and the Cotton Club,
redolent of Dixie-Peach Pomade and Ivory soap,
they jumped 'til the stars disappeared and the roosters woke up.

SHE'S CRAZY WITH THE HEAT

(Helen Jones, Ina Bell Byrd, and Judy Jones on Trombone)

Yeah. You have to hearken to the story behind each song.
That's essential to every good trombone player's art.
To articulate a note, let alone to swing,
trombone players have to feel, and to play from the heart.

So you know the seven positions. That's not enough.
You have to place the notes precisely, so they paint
a picture: bright or dark tones, smooth or rough.
Good trombonists play all over the instrument.

Yeah. The trombone section, in identical gabardine suits,
like dark Betty Grable Rosie the Riveters,
felt their way, tune after tune, to the absolute
unchanging fable of the universe:

That good exists, that love prevails over fear,
that hate and war are eventually kenneled again.
Yeah, our music told this story, to all who could hear.
Yeah: Love will prevail. Yeah. (Don't ask us when.)

RED-HOT MAMA

("Tiny" Davis on Trumpet)

My gal could sweet you to death with her beautiful tone,
then pull you out of yourself to get up and move,
body and soul propelled to a higher plane:
the body to jitterbug, the soul to something like love.

They were rationing food in those days. Every house
with a sunny yard had a "victory" vegetable plot.
My gal washed and ironed (fifty cents a blouse)
and sold sandwiches, to keep herself afloat.

Because times was hard. But all she had to do was blow,
and people of every hue and every age
got caught in a vibration that started with a tapping toe
and rapidly grew into an irresistible urge.

Was part of the population held in internment camps?
Was there a guy you hadn't heard from since before D-Day?
Let the rhythm rule your butt, let the rhythm rule your feet and limbs.
Let yourself acquiesce completely to the music of joy!

THAT MAN OF MINE

("Tiny" Davis on Trumpet)

Musicians walk a tightrope. Below them lie madness and beauty.
The world was aflame, the men soldiering at the front.
The Sweethearts had no philosophy: They just did their duty.
A girl has to trumpet down Jericho, if a man can't.
A girl must fling ecstasy over the world's desperation
with flowery solos, with intricately scattered grace notes,
with hep-cat audacity. She must play a balm for her nation,
with nuanced bravado.
                          Traversing the United States
performing one-nighters, traveling thousands of miles in a year:
the gals had a mission, expressible only in tones.
My gal could quote Satchmo so people stopped dancing to cheer.
Something powerful happened when she and I stepped out alone.
Her pristine technique wove a shimmering texture of sound
that was shot through with joy, on the day Armistice was declared.
Our tender sustained notes! Perfectly inflected whirlwinds!
We constructed a musical edifice out of shaped air
that evening, as if we were charged with high-voltage light.
We played chorus after chorus of "That Man of Mine" that night.

IMPROVISATION, 1948

(Johnnie Mae Rice on Piano)

(The piano remembers.)

(L) A heap of broken images.

          (R) Equal and inalienable rights.

(L) So elegant, so intelligent.

          (R) Recent barbarous acts.

The dead tree gives no shelter.

          Freedom of speech and belief.
          Freedom from fear and want.

The last fingers of leaf.
Fear in a handful of dust.
Hurry up, please, it's time.
And fiddle whisper music.   The conscience of mankind.
          All members of the human family.
          Inherent dignity.
          A common standard of achievement.
          All born free.
          No one subject to torture
          or degrading punishment.
          Equal in dignity and rights.
Dry bones. The river's tent.   The right to seek asylum.
          The right to a nationality.
Departed, have left no address.
Each in his prison thinks of the key.

1948—From the United Nations, a Universal Declaration of Human Rights; Nobel Prize in Literature awarded to poet T. S. Eliot, author of "The Wasteland."

DRUM SOLO, 1950

(Pauline Braddy on Drums)

(The drum-kit remembers.)

Oh, the jukebox jamming
a recorded blare;
oh, the record player:
music everywhere.

Oh, the television,
oh, the brides and grooms,
oh, the male musicians.
Oh, the bare ballrooms.

Oh, the perfect family:
boy, girl, dog, home.
Oh, the undanced rhythms.
Oh, the atom bomb.

A klook a mop, a klook a mop: salt peanuts!
Ragamuffin, ragamuffin. Peach!

THE SONG IS YOU

(Lucille Dixon on Bass)

Musical instruments sleep in the dark
for several hours a day:
the folks we belong to aren't always at play,
so we can't be always at work.

Our silence holds music: an undiscovered bourne,
horizons which have never been viewed,
like undeclared love growing deeper in solitude,
or the crystalline heart of a stone.

My sleep, however, was more like a death:
in the dark of an attic for years;
forgetting my existence, and my glorious career
with the best female swing band on the earth.

I was the great love of my Sweetheart's life.
A man came between us. And soon
I was in the dark collecting dust and out of tune;
they were pronounced man and wife.

Instead of the charts, my gal read Dr. Spock.
We played once a week, once a year . . .
At first, from my closet, I was able to hear
her family's continuo of talk.

My sweetheart's grandson brought me to the shop.
Something has ruined my voice.
Older, not riper, I'm a sorry old bass.
But that doesn't mean I've lost hope

. . . that someone will hold me in a tender embrace,
her arms will encircle my neck;
someone will press her warm length to my back,
and pluck notes from my gut with her fingers' caress.

II. OTHER SELECTED POEMS

From *The Cachoeira Tales and Other Poems*

FASTER THAN LIGHT

For Ohio Wesleyan University Chapter
Phi Beta Kappa, Eta, of Ohio, 2002

I didn't want to pay to park my car,
so I took a taxi to the train station.
New London is an hour's drive away,
but it was the best solution I could find.
After ten miles or so of idle chat
in which my occupation was confessed,
the driver said *he* was a physicist—
As a hobby, he said: Driving was his trade.
Still struggling to connect my seat-belt clasp,
I asked his opinion of an article
I'd skimmed last weekend in the *New York Times*,
about a man who researches time travel.

He made that *pffft* Parisian cabbies make
in early August, when Americans
try to *parlez avec* them at rush hour.
He gave me a long over-the-shoulder glare,
squeezed the steering wheel, and hit the gas.
He said, *He's wrong. The one thing that would work*
is to fly faster than the speed of light,
through a wormhole. The gravitational field
is full of holes: You only have to find
one and be pulled by metagravitational force.
For energy you could use compressed song . . .
(or words to that effect. My memory

isn't what it was ten minutes ago).
He drove with ten white knuckles on the wheel,
his pinched blue right eye looking back at me,
as we took the curves on two screaming tires.
Faster than light travel, that's the secret.

The government's been onto this for years.
There are other planets waiting to be explored.
This one's almost used up: It's time to move.
We won't take people who don't measure up,
our intellectual inferiors.
Let them inherit the earth: We'll take the skies.
(I still couldn't figure out the seat-belt catch.)

The poor and ignorant population grows
so quickly . . . What?! Deny the right to life?
There's a fuckin' holocaust of the unborn!
But some races and cultures lack the gift
of scientific knowledge. It's the dross
of their stupidity which weighs us down
and holds us back. Faster than light travel!
Faster than light travel! The only way!
We hurtled down the turnpike, passing trucks
Faster than light! and cars full of people
driving hell-bent to get to work on time.
Faster than light travel, that's the ticket!

Finally, we pulled up at the train station.
(I'd given up on fastening my seat belt—
stupid contraption—trusting to
the universe to grant me more good luck.)
I scrambled out. We wished each other well.
(My tip was generous, if I do say so myself.)
Faster than light, he yelled, late for his next
pickup, zooming off, talking to his phone.
(My cup brimmed over with Psalm Twenty-Three.
Buoyancy's sometimes stronger than gravity.)
I wheeled my luggage down the crowded train,
then found a seat and opened my magazine.

Some influence is affecting a space probe,
I read, which baffles scientists. It will
rewrite the laws of physics and astronomy
when scientists understand and name that force.

The plan was for *Pioneer 10* to arrive
some million years from now, at some far place.
In case of alien contact, there's a plaque
of a human couple, and a celestial map
showing Earth with a spear held to her head.
Thirty years beyond its launch, it's past Pluto,
the farthest planet orbiting our sun,
in empty space 7 billion miles from Earth.

The article said current theories can't explain
what's causing the decrease in *Pioneer*'s speed.
It's almost imperceptible, a mere
6 mph per century: But *Pioneer 10*
is being pulled back to the sun. I closed my eyes.
. . . *Several million years from now.* As if
a species on the brink of extinguishing itself
said to a future species, *Remember me?*
The species which perfected genocide?
Will Science ever discover humility?
Right, Fool: You want to say en garde *to Science?*
Why stop there? Why don't you attack Knowledge,

while you're at it? And how about Progress?
Ain't that a bit ambitious, Miss William Blake?
What was that voice? Listen, Marilyn, listen:
as saints once listened (and, of course, the mad).
I looked around: The other passengers
were busy with laptops, breakfasts, books.
And where does it get off, accusing me? Ambition?
Why, I've surpassed every fantasy I had.
Would I presume to bad-mouth our attempt
to cheat death? My poems: a handful of dust
trying to get back to supernova.
Like every longing, everything alive.

But ambition wants the immortality
of a members-only country club Valhalla,
an eternal summit meeting of great names.

Millions of light-years into the future,
that immortality ambition breeds
with serendipity: What will it mean?
Our poetry, our books, our language: dust
of words never again to be spoken.
I wonder what *will* last millions of years:
A stone? A nuclear waste storage site?
Will *Homo sapiens* evolve, or die?
Will wiser beings populate our earth?

We're dying faster than the speed of light,
our fame forgettable. Will good deeds, too,
vanish like molecules of exhaled breath,
to be recycled by the universe?
Girl, get on back to the raft. When you try to think,
the breeze between your ears nearly blows me away.
My Muse again. So much for my magazine.
I closed its pages and began to drift.
As if you wasn't drifting all along.
If you had the good sense God promised the carrot,
you'd know that what lasts is the hush of space:
the hiss of orbit, and the hum of stars.

If you could launch a space probe, I wondered,
would you take up my name engraved in gold?
My puny thoughts, my hopes for the future?
And, if I knew I'd be anonymous,
would I publish? Would I write poems at all?
(*During the countdown of* The Anonymous,
you'd be trying to scratch your initials on the hull.)
Well, Muse of Disposable Poetry,
at least I'm not producing toxic waste!
But poets who want immortality,
poets who are ambitious: Is it wrong
to want life after our deaths for our songs?

Leave immortality to cancer cells:
They don't know when to stop. Just when they reach

the point of no return, the body dies,
and the cancer is returned to genesis.
Genes are programmed to reproduce and die;
and poetry, to stick on a synapse,
lucky to be a line remembered wrong.
Your work, projected into the future,
is pulled back to earth by dark energy,
the glue which binds the cosmos together . . .
From Stamford I no longer traveled alone:
my seatmate fast-talked into his cell phone.

CACHOEIRA TALES

Life is nothing but stories.
> —Albert J. Price, Captain, Ret., American Airlines

GENERAL PROLOGUE

When April rains had drenched the root
of what March headlines had foreseen as drought,
I invited my extended family—
with artificial spontaneity—
to join me on some kind of "pilgrimage."
A fellowship gave me the privilege
of offering to cover their airfare
and several nights in a hotel somewhere.
Thinking of a reverse diaspora,
I'd planned a pilgrimage to Africa.
Zimbabwe, maybe, maybe Senegal:
Some place sanctified by the Negro soul.

My brother Mel's response was, "What the hey:
I'll go to Timbuktu, if you're going to pay."
My sister Jennifer said, "What's the catch?
It's not like you to offer a free lunch."
I put on my most innocent who-me? look:
No catch. (I planned to use them in this book.)
So she agreed. We vetoed Zimbabwe
because of Mugabe. We couldn't stay,
as I'd hoped, in a village on a farm,
and I might put us in the way of harm
if I took them to the Mizeki Festival,
which honors the black Anglican who fell,
martyred by the spears of his kinspeople.
My option was to fly to Senegal
and visit *L'Abbaye de Keur Moussa.*
I priced a round trip to Dakar: *Py-ha!*
Impossible. Unless we didn't eat . . .
Maybe the monks would put us up gratis . . .

I checked their website. Well, so much for that!
So far, my pilgrimage was falling flat.

I consulted the map: Jamaica? Trinidad?
I'd have to modify the plan I had
concocted on the fellowship application,
but at least we'd have a wonderful vacation.
But, except for visiting Bob Marley's grave
to contemplate his brief, amazing life,
and connecting with Jah in the incense of a joint,
this option offered no apparent point.

Then my son Jacob e-mailed from Brazil,
where he's studying at a Bahian school.
He'd found an inexpensive online fare
from L.A., New York, or Miami to Salvador.
We could fly down to Bahia, visit him,
and go to *A Igreja do Bonfim,*
a church on a hill overlooking All Saints' Bay,
sacred to Christians and followers of Candomblé.

We met at JFK. From there we flew
to Salvador together, along with two
other Americans of slave descent.
The following describes the friends who went
together, and the friends we met en route,
simplifying each to a major attribute.

The DIRECTOR of a small black theater
was there. She had decided to be poor,
if that's what it would take to live for art.
She'd spent three decades following her heart's
uncompromisingly high principles,
making aesthetic and political
choices of scripts and casts. For thirty years
she'd paid her dues to craft, and watched her peers
and some less talented become rich shills,
or extras with homes near Beverly Hills

and a taste for cocaine. Her great reviews
didn't increase her theater's revenues:
Black audiences crowded the multiplex,
preferring violence and packaged sex;
white audiences stayed away in droves.
She coveted a car that worked, nice clothes,
and the guilt-free personal luxury.
She could *be* the lipless game-show M.C.
the night the black lady knew the answers,
could *be* George W., in just a couple of glances.
She was an ample sister, middle-aged,
a champagne cocktail of faith and outrage,
with one tooth missing from her ready smile,
a close Afro, and a bohemian style.

A JAZZ MUSICIAN came along, as well.
He was the kind of charmer who can sell
drummers insurance. His life's odyssey,
from cutting high school classes regularly
to play the blues, through touring with a band,
through playing for a circus in Japan,
had filled him with good-humored confidence.
In a previous life he might have been a prince,
waving aside the suck-ups and the phonies,
recognized as a man with great *cojones.*
His mother-tongue was music: He spoke bass,
flute, and piano, and was of that race
which strives to make work "fit for the plateau."
His California cool, go-with-the-flow
attitude was a most endearing trait,
except that it made him tend to sleep late,
which irritated people less laid-back.
His motto was the universal black
shrug to those who'd make tardiness a crime:
"You have the watches, but we have the time."
He hummed, drummed on tables, and laughed a lot.
Thinking of himself as a polyglot

in training, he improvised Portuguese
as he had French, Spanish, and Japanese.
Cigarettes seemed to be his only vice.
But life's a crapshoot played with loaded dice.

The retired PILOT had also held a seat
in the state legislature. A complete
Morehouse man, urbane, witty, and astute,
he had been taught early to elocute
and. he. spoke. clearly. every I.N.G.
He had a deep passion for history,
the disposition of a raconteur,
and the palate of a true connoisseur.
He'd served on the board of the W.C.C.
and was committed to philanthropy.
A worn copy of Emerson's essays
was the last thing he took from his suitcase.
He wore a Greek fisherman's cap and drank
bourbon. He had the dignity of rank
and the habit of looking at his watch,
and when there was no bourbon he drank scotch.
He had eleven siblings, disowned ten,
divorced and was never married again.
But he'd set his children on the right track:
Both were professionals, proud to be black.
He ordered wine with dinner when he could,
tasting, and then pronouncing it "Damn. Good."

You can spend decades playing by the rules,
counting your blessings, praise in every pulse,
raising your children, making a career,
and have your dearest blessings disappear—
like that. You can tell me it was bum luck
that made a mother stagger thunderstruck
from one hospital bed to the other,
carrying messages between brothers.
But I think God had made another bet,

and won. Maybe God's not satisfied yet
that quality tests of the human soul
have proved the Sixth Day wasn't just a whole
waste of Her precious time; that faith exists
like Job's . . .
                    We were joined by an ACTIVIST,
who had been struck by double tragedy
and had broken a killing secrecy
by making "Danny's House" in Washington, D.C.,
home to programs on AIDS and HIV.
By serving is one comforted;
by tossing stones into the river's bed
one can change the current of history.
She was planning an autobiography
about the years she spent in the Peace Corps,
about the NAACP and CORE,
about finding her mother . . . I won't paint
the details here. (Her friends say she's a saint.)
And here she was, rediscovering the world:
a certain-age beauty, wide-eyed as a girl.

Now I have thumbnail-sketched the company
of interesting people who went with me,
and who are now (a different now) sitting
around a table, telling side-splitting
stories, which just unfold in the exchange.
I interrupt, suggesting we arrange
a little competition, with a prize.
Everyone turns, with are-you-kidding? eyes.
Then they turn back, and the pilot tells the rest
of the one about the brother taking the Rorschach test:
"So the shrink says, 'My goodness, Mr. Green,
your have the filthiest mind I've ever seen!'
The brother says, 'It's just like the white man
to blame the Negro! Dr. Smith, you can
say what you want, but you got to admit you're
the one that showed me all them dirty pictures!'"

C.I.A.

Over *moqueca,* rice and beans, we talked
about the narrow winding streets we'd walked,
about shopkeepers waving us to stop,
and how rich we felt walking into a shop
and dropping three dollars for something we loved.
We talked about those Stellas with they groove,
about how friendly the Bahians seemed.
The jazz musician said, "Yet not extreme.
I've witnessed extreme friendliness abroad.
And let me tell you, it was pretty weird.

"My band had booked a gig on a cruise ship,
playing top 40s and getting great tips
for sneaking Sinatra in once in a while.
When we docked, we were free to explore the isle.
I'd walk around, or rent a motorbike,
or if I was feeling ambitious, take a hike.
On every island, once or twice a day,
someone would sidle up to me and say,
'Hello, my brother! (Are you C.I.A.?)'
I'd say I wasn't, and they'd walk away.
By the sixth island, it would have been dense
to think this might be a coincidence.
I asked an asker if he could tell me why
so many people thought I was a spy.
'Aw, Mon,' he said. 'Was you born yesterday?
If you want good dope, you go to the C.I.A.!'
I don't remember that island as well as the rest:
I sold some national secrets and had a blast!"

HARMONIA AND MOREEN

A man's eyes, when a young Bahiana walks
—saunters? parades? or better: undulates—
when a young Bahiana undulates past him
(back-straight, up-tilting, with sun-gilded limbs

and a butt like twin scoops of *doce de leite* ice cream)
a man's eyes light up; he snorts puffs of steam.
The old Bahianas, in white eyelet shirts,
the Saints' bright beads, and long white eyelet skirts,
sit by bubbling cauldrons in *acaraje* stands,
scooping shrimp into fritters. With a glance,
men dismiss them; they take a bite and pay.
The old Bahianas watch them walk away.

We heard them first, then met two sisters from home:
Harmonia and her sidekick, Moreen.
They were retracing the diaspora:
they'd just finished doing West Africa;
Jamaica and Haiti were coming next.
Were they wealthy? Or was this the pretext
of two very deep undercover spies?
It might have been a James Bondian disguise:
Just think of the movie possibility:
Two sisters, keeping it safe to be free.
They wore outfits bought on the continent:
Harmonia a turquoise and green print
with matching head wrap, Moreen black and red
with lots of cowries clinking in her dreads.
"You know black people always been wanderers,
but God made us too poor to pay the fare,"
Moreen said, in some kind of secret code
she acted like we were supposed to know.
Harmonia cried, "Yes, girl! That's the truth!"
She poked me with one elbow. "Ain't it the truth?"
Moreen went on: "Negro got put out of line
for first-day gifts at the beginning of time,
because he was looking at White Woman funny.
That's why black folks don't have no money
but we all over the globe. Say amen!
Black folk arrived on the American
part of this planet like seeds riding birds.
Honey, frankly, I wouldn't give two turds
for that piece of desert they fighting about over there.

Somebody need to teach they ass to share!"
Moreen high-fived Harmonia's lifted hand.
"Seem like they need *another* Promised Land!
Seem like some bearded white man with a hat
could prove that if you carefully retranslate
one letter of scripture, you can see God say
the Promised Land's someplace in Uruguay."
Harmonia threw up her hands and screamed.
Then she did a little dance around Moreen.

BAIXA MALL

Our third day promised intermittent showers,
but we're Americans: We can spend hours
in malls, purchasing more of what we have,
on high-interest credit—self-sold slaves
to globalized corporate usury,
chained by ads which insist we're free.
And I *needed* cosmetics, underwear,
a T-shirt. And we *needed* souvenirs . . .
So we took two taxis to the Baixa Mall.
It felt almost like home: the bustling aisles
full of the energy of market day,
vendors marketing wares from far away.
But the trademarks weren't familiar, and the crowds
were every color of the brown rainbow.
And we couldn't believe the low prices:
It was like holding a hand of aces!
The dollar towered over the *real*
like a gun-toting Hollywood cowboy.
The rich must feel like this, spending money
like fountains of beneficence. Honey,
let me tell you, it felt right nice! We ate
in the food court on the Styrofoam plates
we knew from home, though some of the tastes were new.
From the far side of the hall, a loud halloo
called our attention. Harmonia and Moreen!
Moreen in peach, Harmonia in aubergine.

They ran to join us, carrying plastic bags
that slapped against their thighs. "Girl, are we glad
to see ya'll!" Harmonia cried. "We loved ya'll's plan
to get the Man to move the Promised Land!"
Moreen said, "How about this exchange rate!
I feel like I'm lugging around some great
BIG money! Like the time ol' Anansi
wanted a beautiful woman to see
he was *muy macho,* so he switched his tool
for the tool of his friend, the elephant bull.
Now, you know Trickster's small: He had to haul
that thing around, while he waited for the girl.
At first, he let it drag along the ground,
but it hurt, and it tripped him up. He found
it easier to toss it over one shoulder,
though it was like carrying a gold boulder.
When he finally traded back his instrument,
he'd learned something about greed, and good sense.
All this giant money, like a huge tool,
and all them rich people acting the fool
with elephant ding-dongs around their necks,
when a signature on one of their personal checks . . . "
Harmonia cleared her throat and gestured.
"Have you met our guide? I tell you, sisters,
he's the cutest white man I've ever seen!
We have to go." She left, dragging Moreen.

Shrugging, we watched the trio disappear.
What was that gadget in that white man's ear?
We shopped more, then went back to our hotel
to kill some more time checking our e-mail.
Then, after a large meal and the local drink
of rum, sugar, and lemons, still half drunk
with the power of dollars, we relaxed
around a game of conversation catch.
The pilot tossed a high one: During his service
as a board member of the World Council of Churches,
he often traveled on the continent,

and was asked the same two questions wherever he went.
The first question he was asked invariably
was, "You're American? Do you really
have twenty-five different kinds of toothpaste?"
The second, in West Africa or East,
in North or South—and he swore this was true—
was, "Do whites read the same Bible we do?"

"Toothpaste," we echoed. We grew serious,
remembering Africa, which most of us
had visited at least once in our lives.
We sipped our drinks, exchanging narratives:
The director and her daughter taken in,
like long-lost, new-found, much-beloved kin,
by a woman who befriended them in Dakar,
who cooked meals for them on a charcoal fire
behind her house, and pushed the money away
when the director had offered to pay
for her and her family's hospitality.
At last there was an opening for me:
I told about the tranquil week I spent
in the Manger Sisters' Harare convent,
how much I enjoyed kneeling with the nuns
as they prayed the canonical hours with drums.
They fed the poor with produce from their farm
in a remote village. Their order, formed
by a black nun, was all black, one of few
black Catholic religious orders I knew
of, the Oblate Sisters of Providence,
formed in 1829, the oldest.
Its foundress, a free woman, Mother Mary Lange,
was a refugee from the rise of Toussaint
and Haiti's full-blood blacks against the whites
and their mulatto offspring, born of rapes.
Haitian mulatto refugees fled north
and wound up free blacks in the American South,
seventy years before the Civil War.
Mary told her confessor, Père Joubert,

that God was calling her to start a school
and to dedicate her life by taking the veil.
So these should-be candidates for sainthood
collected funds for a girls' school which would
have a curriculum of the classics,
vocational training, art, and music.

Their chapel, not exclusively for blacks,
reserved for their white friends two pews in back.
They took in wash and scrubbed floors on their knees
to take in black orphans and widows. These
domestic talents led their archbishop
to order them to be maids, and desist
from the proud sin of thinking they were nuns . . .

The director said, "Is this more of your monk
stuff? Have you been sprinkled with monkey dust,
or something?" She led the laughter of the rest.
(I remembered how I burned her paper dolls;
how I woke up one summer dawn to call,
"It's Christmas!" so she staggered down the stairs
and woke to disappointment and my jeers.
Fifty years later, she's still getting me back
for the way I teased her about her black
favorite doll, which I said was ugly—
or, as we used to say, it was "spoogly"—
"Look at that spoogly ol' black doll!" I'd scream
with my *Little House* and *Little Women* dreams,
my brain washed white as snow . . .)
                                    But I digress.
Where was I? Oh, yes, Africa. The jazz
musician, in Zimbabwe years ago,
was ridiculed because he didn't know
Shona or Ndebele. He was black
so everyone expected him to speak
one of their languages. At last, their fun
made him decide to simply make up one.
"Uhuru ti matata," he said, lifting

his glass to each of them, and then sipping
the local brew. All of the laughers froze.
"What did you say?" they asked. "Oh, you don't know
Swahili," he said, with his eyebrows raised.
"You know Swahili?" They were all amazed,
Swahili being the rough equivalent
of French in Africa. "A dialect,"
he shrugged. "Creole Swahili." They were stunned.
They asked if many black Americans
spoke Swahili. The jazz musician laughed.
"I told them, 'Only in the eastern half
of the country; the rest speak Yoruba.'
They pulled chairs close and waved to the bar.
'Teach us.' For several hours I drank their beers
and taught them a language invented between my ears."

My son said that Bahians know the tribes
of their ancestors and have kept alive,
in chants, phrases, and words, the languages
they prayed in during the Middle Passage.
Their gods survived by putting on white masks,
so slaves could answer, when their masters asked,
"We pray, as you have taught us, to the One,
to His white saints, and to His Jewish son."

The Christian saints became the Orishas:
Yemanja-Mary, Oxala-Jesus . . .
Or was it vice-versa? We paused to think,
meanwhile ordering another round of drinks—
two lemons squeezed, a scoop of sugar, rum,
shaken, not stirred, served over ice—and *yum!*
We drew near the point of feeling no pain.
The ball fell in the pilot's court again.
He told about flying into a coup
somewhere: I think it was Ouagadougou.
He was ordered to taxi to the gate,
keep the doors locked, take no pictures, and wait.
He shoved his camera underneath his seat

and sat there sweltering in the tropical heat.
Whose funds paid for those guns? He didn't care;
all he wanted was his butt back in the air.
Aloft again, after hours of red tape,
he thought, "Thank God my ancestors escaped."

The bar man brought another round of drinks
and cleared away the empties. Were those winks
between him and the pilot? Possibly.
The jazz musician's volubility
took great leaps forward. Here and there, a word
was garbled, consonants were slurred.
We talked about bureaucracy and greed,
rampant corruption, bribes, visible need,
the land's intractability, the snakes,
the ignorance, the beauty, how dawn breaks
on people already up and about,
how the full moon rises over the veldt.
I met a young woman near Victoria Falls,
one morning on my constitutional,
a basket on her head, her baby tied high
so it peeked over her shoulder. Her eyes,
as we approached each other, watched the road.
My spoken greeting startled her; her load
slipped off her head. I saw, in slow motion,
her momentary loss of composure:
she turned to catch it, and the baby fell,
headfirst, out of its sling. Some miracle
made it fall right into my hands. I felt
like Holden Caulfield, in spite of my guilt—
for I'd averted a near-tragedy,
which almost happened, almost caused by me.
That woman's humble, wet-eyed gratitude
couldn't convince me I'd done something *good*.

The activist said, "What about those nuns?
Did Mother Mary Lange stick by her guns?
Did lightning strike the bishop? I won't sleep

a wink tonight, unless I know what hap-
pened." I told her she was obedient.
Seeing the bishop's order as expedient,
she and her sisters hired out as maids.
Their earnings from their cleaning service paid
to keep widows and orphans housed and fed,
and they held school at night. When Mary died,
they knew she was one of the Ancestors.
"How come she's not a saint?" asked the director.
The jazz musician said, "She is." He yawned.
"I'm bushed. Okay, let's have a show of hands:
who's for hitting the sack, and sleeping in
tomorrow? I could use a vacation
from my vacation: Gimme some time to chill!"
We acquiesced. Good night, sleep tight, Brazil.

OLODUM

> "Where there is dancing, there is hope."

Jake had to take some books back up to CRIA,
where teens study Brazilian *poesia*
and read bits of translated poetry.
(The apple didn't fall far from the tree.)
And Olodum was playing later that night;
we shouldn't miss them: They were dynamite,
he said. So, in the middle afternoon,
we rode to Pelhourino. Olodum,
a band of drummers, was an important part
of that section's renewal, using art
as a hammer to reshape poverty
into a thriving tourist industry.
We walked again along the treeless streets,
past vendors of souvenirs, ribbons, gum, sweets,
and fragrant *acaraje*. Musicians played;
youths performed *capoeira*. Our parade
of tourist dollars was welcomed again
by vendors who remembered us as friends:

"My friends!" they called in English; "I love you!"
We spent more money. What else can you do?
We sought refuge in the St. Francis church,
whose gilt interior invited us to search
for gargoyle cherubs angry slaves had carved
for lazy, fat-cat Christians, while they starved.
Some were still grimacing. But the hard-ons
the guidebooks mentioned all seemed to be gone.
The activist suggest daintily
that a restroom was needed urgently.

We hastened out to search for a café.
The director told a story on the way:
"This friend of mine told me she had to pee
immediately, once, while she was ski-
ing down a Colorado mountainside.
She had to go so badly, she decide-
ed to pull over in a clump of pines
and do her thing. She skied to the tree line,
hid, lowered her pants, and squatted. As she sighed
two relieved clouds of steam, she started to slide
backwards, out of the trees. She couldn't stop;
she skied up a large mogul. In the drop-
off coming down the other side, she fell
and sprained her knee. The vigilant ski patrol
travoised her to a waiting ambulance.
Supine, she struggled to pull up her pants,
wondering why they were just idling there.
Some time later, the ski patrol reappeared
with a young man who had broken his arm.
After they'd gotten him settled and warm,
as they sirened down the curvaceous mountain road,
she asked him how he'd fallen. He replied
that a bare-assed woman skiing backward
had sped toward him; in order to avoid
colliding with this sight beyond belief,
he'd swerved without looking, and hit a tree."

We took turns. Then we took turns ordering
our dinners: Wine, of course, and rice and beans,
Brazil's famous *feijoada*. As we raised
our glasses to the pilot's daily praise—
"Well, the trip has been great, *so far*"—we heard
a familiar commotion, and the birds
of paradise were borrowing two chairs
from other tables, to pull up to ours.
"You all certainly do know how to throw
a party," said Harmonia. Closing
her eyes, raising her hands, for once Moreen
seemed speechless, momentarily. We ate;
they ordered, waited, said grace over their plates,
and joined the general gusto. "Lord, these beans
are better than my mama's," said Moreen.
"I eat them every chance I get. Too bad
ol' ass can't whistle." After we'd ha-ha'd,
she added, "Of course, y'all know why it can't.
. . . How can y'all be black, and so ignorant?
(I thought, "Good question!") "Well," she said, "I'll tell
you, since you asked. It was during a spell
of bad hunting. Trickster shot a gazelle
at the end of another hungry day.
He made a fire, spitted the meat, and lay
with his back to the fire, to take a nap.
He told his ass to stay awake, keep watch,
and whistle a warning if it saw a thief.
Then Trickster closed his eyes and fell asleep.
A jackal skulked out of a nearby bush.
The ass whistled. It fled. Trickster said, 'Hush!
Ain't nothing there!' And he went back to sleep.
Two jackals came. The ass whistled: 'Peep! Peep!'
They fled. Trickster woke up. 'I told you, *hush!*
Ain't nothing there!' His breath became the shush
of sleep again. Three jackals. The ass peeped.
Trickster awoke, furious, out of deep sleep,
and looked around. 'You *double-expletive* liar!'

he yelled, 'Take this!' And he sat down in the fire,
to punish ass for crying wolf. Poor ass
got badly burnt. That's how it come to pass
that ass can't whistle. When it tries . . ." Moreen
puckered her lips. We roared like libertines.

The enclosed plaza where Olodum plays
was crammed with colors, from café au lait
to Hershey's Kisses (trademark) and pigs' feet,
a crowd that overflowed into the street
and down the block. The only tickets left
were sold by scalpers guilty of horse theft
with their outrageous prices. But we paid,
to be shoehorned in and gallimaufried.
Joined skin to skin, we moved like molecules
in the great, impossible miracle
of atmosphere, swaying to the music,
all eyes on the stage, all hearts attuning
themselves in beautiful polyrhythmy,
one shaking booty. On one side of me
a young man danced; I felt his muscled warmth
flow into mine, his pure, sexual strength.
On my other sides young women danced, whose curves
bumped me softly, dancing without reserve,
hands waving in the air, releasing scent
fragrant as nard. We danced in reverent,
silent assent to the praise-song of drums.
The singers sang in Portuguese, but one
repeated English phrase I understood:
"If Jesus were a black man . . ." In the crowd,
one molecule remembered a long, loud,
sixties party, where several of her friends
from different African countries took turns
playing a Quaker's Oatmeal box, surprised
that the rhythms meant the same things to their tribes.
The drums talk. Is there no Rosetta Stone
by which to translate their names for the One

whose dark faces mask Divine Radiance?
I thought I understood, then: They said *Yes.*
God doesn't prefer one language, one gesture,
one form of prayer, one praying posture;
God doesn't prefer the ascetic's self-denial
to the delighted joy-dance of the child.
Half of the families in Brazil earn less
then $4,000 a year. There are estimates
that eight to ten million children live in the street.
Yes, say the drums; *yes,* say the hips and feet,
dancing to sacred music. Levity
celebrates life's one-drumbeat brevity—

A IGREJA DO NOSSA SENHOR DO BONFIM

Bags packed, my siblings agreed to squeeze in,
to shut me up, a trip to the Bonfim
Church, though we might need a police escort
with sirens to get us to the airport
to make our flight back to the U.S.A.
The pilot and the activist would stay
in the hotel until their Rio plane.
So we four set off, to fulfill the plan
for which I'd won my fellowship. The man
who drove our taxi understood our need:
Instead of taking major roads whose speed
was slowed by rush-hour traffic, he cut through
the neighborhoods where tourists seldom go.
Clusters of uniformed children walked to school.
Workers waited for buses, crisp and cool-
looking. (They'd come home wilted by the heat,
after a day of smiling.) Every street
we drove on or caught glimpses of was clean.
Shopkeepers unlocked doors, and laid out green
vegetables and many colors of fruit.
I thanked God we'd been forced to take this route,
to look into open windows and doors.

This was a world we would not have explored,
a world with no neon and no street lights,
a world which makes tourists feel discrete fright,
"But I'm not racist; one of my best friends . . ."
I told them about the time my eyes were cleansed.

I'd gone to Mexico, on sort of a whim,
to join a week-long seminar program
offered by the Sisters of Guadalupe.
I'd gone alone, but was there with a group
of gringo students and their chaperones.
My reason for being there wasn't entirely known
to them or me. Especially to me.
It stemmed more from *eros* than from *agape*.
We breakfasted in silence every day,
then met in the sunny oratory to pray.
They prayed. I gazed out over the landscape:
a steep arroyo and a barren sweep
of sagebrush and cactus. Our days were spent
on lectures about poverty. Or we went
into the homes of the hospitable poor.
We sat on their up-turned pail furniture,
exchanged life stories and farewell blessing.
Each day more humbled by our possessing
so much of the earth's power, I felt sad
and powerless. Late in the week we made
a trek to an arroyo, down and out,
and across land caught in a perpetual drought.
We followed a mile-long extension cord
to a village built of tin and billboards,
where chickens, dogs, and children ran in the dust.
The Sisters greeted people, introduced
their visitors, inquired about health
and gardens. I experienced my wealth
acutely, painfully. At evensong
I saw, where I'd been gazing all along,
that village: right there, in front of my eyes.

I, who had been blind, could now recognize
the individual homes of people I'd met.
That was an awakening I shall not forget.

At the church, descended upon by a swarm
of vendors, we showed the ribbons on our arms
and, shaking our heads to trinkets, rushed inside
to see the room described in all the guides:
walls festooned with emblems of prayers answered.
Snapshots of people who've survived cancer,
unneeded crutches . . . An awesome display.
Then I rushed into the sanctuary to pray,
quickly, that all of us would meet good ends.
I turned: My brother signaled with one hand;
we ran back to our taxi. As we sped
down highways toward the airport, my son said,
"The Lord of Bonfim is both Oxala,
a long-ago king in West Africa,
and Christ. One day Oxala put on rags
to disguise himself, and went with a bowl to beg.
He hoped to see how his people lived, to find
and scourge the cruel, and reward the kind.
Arrested for vagrancy, he was thrown in jail.
Not knowing where he was, no one brought bail.
He sat for years in solitude and filth,
meditating on poverty and wealth.
At last his son Oxossi happened to pass
the miserable jail and see Oxala's face.
His long-lost father, given up for dead!
The king lives! Oxala was quickly freed
and, bathed with honors, returned to his throne.
He said, 'I have learned with my flesh and bones
the conditions under which my people live.
The waters which bathed me are going to give
comfort to those who suffer, and to quench
the fires of greed, injustice, and violence.'
From that day forth, Oxala's kingdom thrived;

he was known as the wisest king who ever lived.
There's a huge procession once a year to wash,
with scented water, the steps of the church,
in honor of Oxala and his twin,
the Christian Christ: both Lords of the Good End."

Our pilgrimage ended, we left Salvador.
Meanwhile, our President cheered us toward war—

TRIOLETS FOR TRIOLET

For the people of a Creole village called Triolet
on the Indian Ocean island nation of Mauritius

I

Walk through the winding streets of Triolet,
its two-room cement houses, whose tin roofs
seem one bright blaze from satellites miles away.
Walk through the winding streets of Triolet:
Watch as dust rises over children's play.
Maids and cane-cutters come home here to laugh.
Walk through the winding streets of Triolet,
who see you, too. Who know you steal their life.

II

Trying to stop, screeching toward Triolet,
the Twentieth Century Express.
. . . A deaf child, lost in reverie or play . . .
Trying to stop, screaming toward Triolet,
your selfishness. Or *ours*. For, I must say,
I'm the Fisherman's Wife, wishing excess.
. . . Wheels sparking, screeching toward Triolet . . .
We hear it, gorging on food we don't bless.

III

Without a history, people stumble
around the grindstone in a deepening track.
Which great-grandparent does this child resemble?
Without their history, people stumble
in Triolet, trying not to remember
that they are poor, unalphabeted, black
and historyless. Brown people stumble
along dirt streets, one lost soul to each block.

IV

Pray for a God-forsaken Motherland,
a ravished Eden with a thorn-grown gate,
in which the Baobab of Life yet stands.
Pray for a God-forsaken Motherland:
her desert destiny, which seems to end,
but for seeds trusted to the winds of fate.
Pray for our God-forsaken Motherland,
that her seedlings not be crowded out by hate.

V

Our ancestry is ashes on the winds—
the Harmattan, the Khamsin, the Haboob—
blowing from the beginning of the end
of Africa. Blown by her desert winds
blended with the Monsoon, the Bise, the Foehn,
her gene pool, blasted out of solitude.
African slaves were ashes on the winds,
but we survive: one people, many bloods.

VI

Who talk like me? Who dye elect despise?
Who patois, out day home, invite guffaw
and swallow rage? Mask, except foe day eyes,
who talk like me? Who dye elect despise?
Who teacher strive to you row peonize
dim tongue till day white as you toe pee awe?
Who talk lacking? Who die elect despise?
In a bline whirl, who accent be day flaw?

VII

Indigenous to no land, only to chance,
despite world history's struggle to weed us out,
we thrive on two seas and three continents.
We are native to no land mass, but chance

makes us one race, heirs of the drum, the dance,
and the cursed blessing of surviving hurt
indigenous to everywhere. Yes, chance
created us, whose ancestors were bought.

VIII

The hope of chattels in the barracoons
was that their seed would multiply and spread
around the earth; that even octoroons,
remembering chattels in the barracoons,
would feel sad wonder. *Thy weird will be done,*
they prayed. Whom you gave stones instead of bread.
Yet the faith of chattels in the barracoons
was that you are good and just, and are not dead.

III. NEW AND UNCOLLECTED POEMS

MILLIE-CHRISTINE

Millie-Christine McCoy (1851–1912), conjoined twins, born slaves, died free.

I

Millie, the universal loneliness
of singletons, from womb to grave alone,
was not our fate, nor the brief happiness
of self-forgetting love which makes two one.

Our fate: surrender to the great unknown
creating power that created us
to be ourself, to do what must be done.
Now I face a universe of loneliness.

We've lived a unique double consciousness.
Black, female, freak, times two: all our life seen
by the objectifyingly perverse
gape of the "normal," who live and die alone.

Identical, inoperably conjoined,
we have shared one shadow. Yet behind your face,
familiar as my own, hide dreams and pain
I cannot know, and untold happiness.

You sleep and cough. Each breath may be your last.
And your death will be the herald of my own.
We're inescapable intimates, blessed and cursed
with each other, two souls merged into one.

We've amassed a trove of memory's gold coin:
fame, far-flung travels, purchasing Master's house
for our family, performing before the Queen . . .
Our fate was our fusion. Given the choice,
who would choose loneliness?

II

The Ancestors believed twins share one soul,
one boundaryless self-identity,
a paradox of each half's being the whole
undivided individuality.

With different temperaments from infancy,
I've always been duplex, always dual,
always both "I" and, at the same time, "we."
Which indicates that we're not one shared soul.

Touted as "The Eighth Wonder of the World,"
I learned to walk by learning to agree
where my four legs would go. I learned to yield
to boundaryless double identity.

Compromise begets camaraderie.
I played, as I was kidnapped, sold, resold,
exhibited, examined. On the sea
I patty-caked and prattled. We were one whole.

When Master brought Mama to Liverpool,
she fainted, seeing me. The court's decree
declared him owner of the double child
undivided by individuality.

Reunited with my enslaved family,
I was held apart, fed dainties, schooled,
taught the piano. But I wasn't free.
Freedom came battles after America pulled
in two its one shared soul.

III

"Who am I?" asked the re-united states
after the war. As if connected twins
had punched each other bloody, blind with rage,
for reasons they couldn't wholly comprehend.

I supported my widowed mistress and my kin,
by my free wills returning to the stage
to be gawked at by singleton women and men
in freak shows all over the re-united states.

"Who am I?" I asked, mirroring their gaze,
at the same time like them, and unlike them:
a hodgepodge of self-doubt, desires, and praise,
but a freak, a two-headed monster, conjoined twins.

Reconstructing itself, the nation licked its wounds
as industry and expansion, like twin plagues,
spread their poisonous microbes on the winds.
America was still bloody, still blind with rage.

And America trooped to see me. I was amazed
by my power to fascinate all kinds
of "normal" Americans, and by the ways
all of them resembled my freak-show friends.

Ask a freak where identity begins and ends:
Is the midget his height? The fat lady her weight?
No, we are each the horizon of a vast mind,
each called to contribute something great
to our united state.

IV

Welcome, ladies and gentlemen: Step right up!
We who are not as others welcome you
to find the essence behind our handicap
and the compassion beyond your ridicule.

Enter the community of the freak show,
daily facing congenital hardship:
the Mule-Faced Lady, the Limbless Torso . . .
Welcome, ladies and gentlemen: Step right up!

Watch me practice a new four-legged dance step
and rehearse a duet. Watch my four hands sew,
for the giants' wedding, a bridesmaid's gown of crepe.
We who are not as others welcome you.

But much of history is a freak show, too.
Freaks live openly, all over the map.
Examine the things "normal" people do,
and you'll recognize their essential handicap.

Those who exploit innocence, who slay hope;
liars and thieves; the greedy and the cruel;
those who spend their lives inwardly asleep
and who lack compassion are freaks beyond ridicule.
If this isn't true, I am a double fool,
and I ought to tell my other I to stop
judging the world: it's weird, that's all I know.
Hey, listen to the Limbless Torso clap!
Come on in! Step right up!

V

My color trumped by my celebrity,
I toured as "The Two-Headed Nightingale."
With first-class tickets on every journey,
I traveled the sea by steam, the land by rail.

Soon a sophisticate, with the world my school,
I spoke *un peu du Français* with fluency,
and some Español, Italiano, and Deutsch, as well.
My race was trumped by my celebrity.

Meanwhile, back home, Black Codes ruled the cities
and Chinese immigration was curtailed.
The great defeated tribal chiefs exxed treaties,
while I toured as "The Two-Headed Nightingale."

Her Majesty Queen Victoria gave me jewels,
and the Czar drove me in a one-horse droshky,
while Europeans flooded to Ellis Isle,
most of them in steerage for the journey.

And Sanford Dole replaced Queen Lili'uokalani.
I saw, beyond the footlights, a freak world
where normalcy masks unnatural greed.
Sad, I sailed the sea, and came home by rail.

History produces diamonds and coal;
what curses one may be what sets one free.
In family gatherings, I was the brightest belle,
light-footed and warbling in harmony,
aunt, not celebrity.

VI

My birth. My mother. My right hands. My chests.
My violated privacy. My face.
My eyes not hers, my eyes not hers: at least
leave me that closet, in this huge shared house!

My dreams. My doubt. My annoying inner voice.
My moment. My memories of the past.
My putting myself last. My compromise.
My birthday wishes. My hearts in my chests.

My being owned. My being self-possessed.
My girlhood of medical exams masking abuse.
My years of childhood outrage, unexpressed.
My violated privacy. My face.

My powerless gender. My despised race.
My sense of the beautiful. My ugliness.
My faith that everyone's here to be of use.
My mine-alone eyes. My eyes mine alone, at least.

My thanks that I/we are among the blest.
My house, crawling with nephews and nieces,
and the brood of those by whom we were possessed.
My silent smile. My closet, in this shared house.

Outside: the aeroplane, moving-picture shows,
the advent of ready-to-wear shirtwaists,
that colored man who went to the North Pole,
Einstein, the Model-T! My time, too fast.
My deaths, stalking my chests.

VII

Pray I will die before Millie grows stiff,
my heartbeat crushed by iron calipers.
Pray Millie-Christine will depart from life
as we came, side-by-side, through heaven's door.

I'm not afraid. Death's just another tour
to a place so impossibly far-off
no one ever returns. And furthermore,
it has no mail service.
                    She's growing stiff.

In bed we used to talk about the grief
of being the one left behind for hours.
Millie took comfort in her firm belief
that her heart would soon be crushed by calipers.

So this is independence. Lonelier
than we imagined. Heavier to lift
the weight of consciousness, not helped by her.
Pray Aunt Chrissie will soon be freed from life.

The cherubs will be asking for autographs.
Millie's making a place for her sister.
Peace, children. Always be the better half.
We're going side-by-side through heaven's door.

Maybe someday, when I am nothing more
than playbills, three gold rings, and photographs,
we'll be remembered as an Ancestor
(or two). God bless you. Pray I won't be left
long, while Millie grows stiff.

Millie died first; Christine lived on alone for seventeen hours. This poem imagines that
brief eternity. The form of the poem is a modified *rondeau redoublé,* times seven.

A SMALL GOOD NEWS

The first warm day. My left-open front door
invites the wintered-over ladybugs
to find their way outside. Hundreds have died,
awakened too soon by the thermostat
or the late-blazing bulb of my desk lamp.
My vacuum cleaner bag is a mass grave.
The survivors swarm to the source of a breeze,
whispering first green and forsythia.
They cling to the screen door like prisoners
longing through barred windows. They make me think
of refugee camps, of men with forgotten names.
Later today, I'll set my captives free.

LITTLE DIALOGUE WITH THE MUSE

Out of its context, does the Self exist?
Or are we merely products of our time,
history, culture: born to pantomime
stock roles as minor members of the cast
of someone else's drama? Are we dressed
in uniqueness, or are we all the same,
each of us tricked out in a meaningless name?
Once we're erased, how long will we be missed?
How long remembered? *You resemble clouds*
drifting across the pale blue atmosphere.
Does what we've done survive, in a half-life
of infinite decrease, perfect or flawed?
Your work writes on the wind, "Kilroy was here."
The signature of a November leaf.

FIRST ALZHEIMER'S SONNET

A wave enters the membrane labyrinth,
and something mushrooms from nothing to now.
Unacted on, thought disappears from sense
like the vapor trail of a skeptic's awe:
Look up, no trace remains. The road to hell
is paved with good intentions once conceived
of, twice forgotten in a micromill-
isecond, cumulus lost on a breeze.
So what if for a moment the flame burns
higher, as a thought forms of you, my dear,
then *pssses* back into oblivion?
Each cloud is one face of the atmosphere,
as each wave is one aspect of the sea.
Forget you? Never. Not while I am me.

SECOND ALZHEIMER'S SONNET

How many things will I forget today,
how many times stop still and ask myself
what I was going to do? In what new ways
will my mind play tricks on me? What a wealth
of experiences tossed into the wind.
What masterpieces lost even to me.
Without them, am I still one of a kind,
a unique loop of interpreted memory?
How much can one forget—an actor's name,
the novel I finished reading last night,
where the damn car keys are—and still remain
a bubble of identity riding a wave of light?

(*A turd in sewage remembers a meal,*
my Muse remarks. *I am what makes you real.*)

THE TRUCELESS WARS

among beasts, and among men, are worlds apart.
The pigeon lays down fluttering life to flash
a russet tail. The haddock becomes harp seal,
then polar bear. The squirming termite licked
from a sharp stick awakes to invent tools.
The lamb lies down within the lion, yawns
yellow-fanged, and sleeps. Life struggles to evolve
higher in us, through questioning, toward hope.
But we sow salt. We leave a ground-zero wake
of futurelessness. Take the way a life
devolves from thought to blind mouths in the dust,
wasted by semiautomatic fire.
This flesh is foolscap. We think we're so smart,
but we create nothing, nothing. Nothing.

LIVE JAZZ, FRANKLIN PARK ZOO

Kubie sobbed when a nearby jazz band stopped playing.
—*Christian Science Monitor,* August 27, 1996

A tree grew. Oh, remembering gorillas!
O Orpheus singt! Oh, Africa in the ear!
The recluse, Vip, came out. Gigi sat still
and wide-eyed, black face pressed against the bars.

Kubie lay on his back, as he usually does,
vacantly staring. Then he turned over, hairy chin
on one huge leather palm; with his other hand
he scratched his head, contemplatively picked his nose.

The zebras' ears twirled. Behind their fancy fences,
the silenced animals listened to something more.
And where there had been, at most, a nest of boughs
to receive it, music built a cathedral in their senses.

TO THE CONFEDERATE DEAD

We shall say only the leaves
Flying, plunge and expire.
            —Allen Tate, 1928

On the way to Nashville my cell-phone rings
on I-24. I take the next exit
and return the missed call. Then see the sign:
Beech Grove Confederate Cemetery. I turn in,
pass a white house, drive up a hill, and stop.
The Stars and Bars wave over white headstones.
Beyond, a verdant pastoral.

I park the rental, leave my purse and keys,
and read the markers. *Hoover's Gap.*
Here the 17th Tennessee Infantry
met the 18th Indiana Battery
on June 24, 1863.
I do not count the headstones,
the identical headstones.
Unknown Confederate Soldier.
One after one, after one. Three rows.

Spencer repeating rifles, three-inch
ordnance rifles, mountain howitzers,
and this bucolic landscape.
The 17th marched here in the rain
that morning, to a mounted infantry
led by a man whose name rings a bell:
Capt. Eli Lilly.
He made his own history.

A framed statement of patriotic nostalgia
displayed near the flagpole
makes me wonder what it was
about the old South
these nameless dead

loved enough to die for.
Was it really slavery?
Did they despise
my people enough
to want to die
to keep us in chains?
Even the boy who groaned here
remembering a molasses-skinned girl
who was his in the cabins?
The boy who knew he was hers
as her name shaped his last breath?
Even the boy who moaned Mammy
remembering dark mothering arms?
Did he die
so someone could sell her children?

Left behind by history's tides
like bodies tossed overboard,
what did these unknown learn
as the bullets shattered through them?
Did they suddenly know
our common humanity?
Did arrogant ignorance
bleed away?

Engraved on granite, the farewell speech
of General Nathan Bedford Forrest:
... *CULTIVATE FRIENDLY FEELINGS* ...
My ancestor, Henry Ashburne Tyler,
was one of Bedford's Raiders.
He fathered my great-grandfather and his sister,
and gave their mother a house.
His legitimate children died
without issue. His only
descendants are us:
a college president, teachers,
professors, a pilot, accountants,
business people, musicians,

an actor, some writers,
good people. People who feel blessed.
Would he be proud
of us?

I am awakened from my musings
by the crunch of tires on gravel.
White men. Five of them.
They pass very, very, very slowly,
staring.
Then they turn around and squeal away.

You were boys, I say aloud.
You were boys.
I get back in my car
and drive on to Nashville.

BIVOUAC IN A STORM

A Tuskegee Airmen story

Biloxi, Mississippi, Keesler Field:
The only place on earth where you can be
up to your knees in mud and coughing dust,
the brothers laughed, marching in summer heat
thick as blackstrap molasses, under trees
haunted by whippings, dripping Spanish moss.
Pre-aviation basic training. Drill
in armed and unarmed combat, bayonets
and rifles, obstacle courses; to see
the group as one, killing or being killed,
brothers in blood and courage, fear and sweat,
challenged to be all a black man can be.

The air cadets, sent out to bivouac
under glowering clouds, quick-stepped through swamps,
some corpuscles remembering bloodhounds,
some synapses alert for coral snakes.
They reached dry ground at dusk, and set up camp.
They cooked and ate, and were sitting around
shooting shit as distant thunder rolled,
when a rumble of boots and a clash of arms
announced a detachment of regular
Army: one hundred soldiers, all white boys.
White boys from Midwest small towns, Southern farms,
and Northern cities. White boys with one glare.

Their detachment leader told the *niggers* to scram.
Shit, man, whispered. The brothers pitched their tents
in a boggy meadow and waited out the storm.

A blinding flash awoke them, a raw *BLAM!*
One scream, forged of one hundred man-screams blent
into one terror, made the brothers form
a gaping mass aghast at the rain of sparks,
the flying body parts, the agonies,

the pain, the fear beyond the thunder's roar,
up there, for one breath. Then they flew to work
in the deluge, through mud up to their knees,
breathing the ozone energy of war.

Lightning had struck the hill; the white boys' cache
of ammunition. Several boys were dead.
When Daddy told this, I started to laugh.
But he looked at the floor and shook his head.

SIX-MINUTE DOGFIGHT

Clarence "Lucky" Lester, July 18, 1944
A Tuskegee Airmen story

On a plate-glass-window, ceiling-unlimited morning,
a squadron of Mustangs scrambles into the sky
to a rendezvous at 25,000 feet
over Umbrian villages and the lie of peace.
Despite his sheepskin jacket, Lester shivers,
more from anticipation than from the cold.
The pilots of the bombers he's escorting
might refuse to shake his hand, but what the hell:
homefolk Chicago teachers write to him
and send kids' crayon drawings signed with love.

Black dots emerging from blue clarity
develop into Messerschmitt 109s,
and Lester closes to 200 feet,
thumbing his fire button to release
an ack-ack burst of steel. The Hun explodes.
A second Hun buzzes in at three o'clock;
Lester banks right and fires. A tail of smoke
follows its spinning dive, a parachute
blossoming down there at 8,000 feet
as another swastika howls down in flames.

A third bandit, riding Lester's tail,
shoots gray lines past him. Lucky Lester chops
his throttle, falls behind, and fires a burst.
The Hun rolls upside-down, screaming toward green.
The brothers radio verbal high fives,
regroup around the bombers, bring them in,
and take the white boys home. Then, back on earth,
where a hero can still be a second-class citizen,
they congratulate each other and mourn their lost.
Lester is awarded the Distinguished Flying Cross.

WRITTEN IN CLOUDS

For Les Kay, USMC, Vietnam

Now you're a buddy mucking
ten yards away with a rifle,
identical as an armed popcorn
in the enemy's crosshairs, then
you're saying hello darkness.
Now you see,
now you don't.
Is anyone ever ready?
Do you get an explanation?
An apology?
Or does the water that was you,
that was seventy percent of you,
reenter the cycle and shed your name?
Evaporating, condensing, purifying,
quenching, forming ice crystals
and rainbows, the same water
for billions of years recycled
in the planet's breathing helix:
Molecules of this shape-changing skyscape
must once have been you,
Morales. They must have been you,
Woody, Armstrong, Moses.
Doc, Peters, Capadano. Good Marines,
all of you.

HONOR GUARD

Lost in blue stillness, I ride on a wave
of cumulous daydreams. We stand at ease,
whiling away our wait. Some birds call dubs
from the bordering trees. I check my watch.
They're twenty minutes late: He must be loved.
Distant traffic. A breeze tickles the leaves.

Under the cloud scud, a rolling landscape
of white markers in perfectly spaced rows.
I'm brought back from surfing the sky's sea-face
by crunching wheels and the call to attention.
We perform as drilled, precisely synchronized,
the ritual of warriors laying a comrade to rest.

The hearse delivers the flag-draped coffin
into the strict ballet of our white-gloved hands.
The riflemen fire a perfectly timed salute.
As the bugle plays the twenty-four notes of taps,
I glance at the brown knot of the next-of-kin:
probably parents, siblings, his pregnant wife.

Pvt. Joseph Gonzales, of Tucson, was nineteen.
A roadside explosive device. We fold his flag
slowly into a triangle of stars
which the Sergeant presents, with the nation's gratitude,
to the stunned child-bride-widow. The older man
stares into space. The older woman moans
Dios mio, Dios mio, Dios mio, ay Dios mio.

ETERNAL OPTIMIST

A reading of Psalm 87

All find their home in you, Jerusalem,
source of eternal waters, fountainhead, well.
Spiritual umbilicus.
                    Eden
defended and divided by a wall
of bitterness.
                    Yet may the future say:
"Here mankind wisened up. Here peace was born.
The Peoples of the Book suddenly saw,
here, that the chosen are to be the cornerstones
of humanity's grandest vision for the future.
Here peoples united. Here enemies
accentuated what they had in common
and healed the feud in Abraham's family."

May there be princes dancing in your streets,
someday, Jerusalem. May you birth peace.

PSALM FOR ANOTHER PEOPLE

A reading of Psalm 137

By the army checkpoints we sit and weep
when we remember Palestine.
There, near pushed-over olive groves,
we hang our lutes on the barbed-wire fence.
For there the soldiers tell us to sing,
the occupiers demand songs.
They say, "Sing us an Arab folksong!
Dance!"

How can we sing the Lord's song
in a besieged land?
If I forget you, East Jerusalem,
may my right hand forget
how to stroke the strings.
May my tongue cleave
to the roof of my mouth
if I forget you, oh Silwan,
my birthplace, my childhood's joy.

Lord, you heard their words
on the day the bulldozers came.
"Tear down their houses," they shouted;
"Pull their trees out by the roots!
Let them find some other place to live!"

Show your spoiled favorites
hate's self-magnifying mirror:
Blessed be the hands that will dash
their infants against rocks.

NINE TIMES NINE, ON AWE

Florence and Berlin, Summer 2006

I

An architecture of inequity
designs the lower floors of history,
the unchanged, uncountable crypts of misery
where the living and the dead are distinguished by their smell
—one stinks of sweat and shit; one stinks of hell—
and life goes on because lives are replaceable.
Forgotten, those whose years were brief and harsh,
who progressed from the bad to the even worse,
while someone the world would remember was inventing an arch.

II

Always, the cobbled-over vestiges
whisper to what is now of what once was.
Their only explanation is Because.
The relics of uncanonized saints lie
under our sandals, as we hurry by
toward our goal of pizza in a café.
We balance on the shoulders of the great
and the nameless, faceless hordes under their feet,
whose histories whisper from the cobblestone streets.

III

But let us not deny the power of awe:
to stand breathless, gaping, murmuring *wow*
is a modern equivalent of prayer.
We travel across miles and centuries
hoping beauty will knock us to our knees,
lost momentarily in ecstasies.
Is it to *see* we seek, or to *be seen*?
In art's deep inner stillness, do we mean
more than the suffering and brevity of being?

IV

Tourists imagine our lives will be changed
—new DNA, molecules rearranged—
simply by seeing the beautiful, the strange.
In Africa, we tick off the Big Five;
in Europe, we visit works we recognize
from schoolbooks. The works of those who believed
in co-creation, working Hand on hand
with the Creator, make us understand
what the sacred once meant to humankind.

V

Yet tourism can be a way of counting coup.
We e-mail photographs, as if to prove
Kilroy was here, on a Vespa through the Louvre.
Fra Angelico wept. May the sacrament of his tears
open our jaded hearts. No other cures
exist for this contagion of malaise,
except our humble bowing before art.
As they say, art is long, but life is short.
We know we rush to places in the dirt.

VI

Before we take off for the afterworld,
I'll shape this little verse into a gold
circlet around a beloved pate. Behold:
a priest canonized by secular love!
Let's raise an *alleluia* and an *ave*
for the one immortality mortals have:
art's imitation life, *la vie ersatz*.
If a poem has the power to stop the clocks,
here's to brief timelessness for Abba Jacques.

VII

The beautiful is mass-produced today
as cut-rate replicas for the *hoi polloi.*
Does assembly-line uniformity destroy
our experience of awe? Yes, the *David* cloned
moves us less than the one *David* alone.
Machine-made art cannot contain art's pain.
Reproductions cannot hold us rapt
like the illuminated manuscript
an old monk drew out of his prayerful depths.

VIII

We want to care, but the funeral vase
made centuries ago simply because
someone was loved by someone else and lost,
we look at, and forget. Babylon's walls
remind us of a trip to Disney World.
Untutored in the art of seeing well,
we gaze at surfaces and eddy past.
Book learning doesn't change our peasants' taste,
even though we're now upper-middle class.

IX

Guidebooks can't tell us what we ought to feel
in front of Important Works. (Convenient small
full-color photos make it possible
to identify Important Works without wasting our time
on minor strivers.) As a rule of thumb,
however, it can't hurt to be struck dumb.
The awe of the aesthetic experience,
part of our universal inheritance,
makes us basilicas of reverence.

IN THE WAITING ROOM

Homage to Elizabeth Bishop. From a sojourn in Polynesia, where hundreds of
nuclear tests took place in uninhabited regions from 1966–1996. It is believed that
these tests may be related to the elevated levels of thyroid cancer on the nearest
inhabited islands.

In Rikitea, Mangareva,
I went with Aunt Ahuura
to her oncology appointment
and sat in the waiting room.
It was winter. The sea breeze smelled
of ylang-ylang. The waiting room
was full of pareos and tattoos,
tiare and hibiscus behind the ears.
My aunt was inside
what seemed like a long time
and while I waited I read
La Vahine d'Aujourd'hui
(I could read) and carefully
studied the articles:
how to have legs like a gazelle,
how to turn a man on,
a new way to slice avocados.
There were adverts
for hand cream and mozzarella,
for hair conditioner, tampons.
A family sat at table
over corned-beef-stuffed breadfruit.
Taste Scotland, the caption read.
Ladies with short hair and red, red lips,
ladies with visible ribs,
like wire sculptures
hung with coconuts.
Their breasts were horrifying.
I read it straight through.
No *tabu* made me stop.
And then I looked at the cover:
the pale model, the date.

Suddenly, from inside,
came an *oh!* of pain
—Aunt Ahuura's voice—
that meant Bad News.
She had almost whispered
since the surgeon removed
one wing of her voice.
Hearing her so clearly
was shock enough, but what took
me completely by surprise
was that it was *me:*
my voice, in my mouth.
Like the prophetess Toapere,
I was the entire *ohana,*
all of our people, and we were falling, falling,
sliding off a timeless canvas
into Today, into Now.

I said to myself: You are ten, born
years after the nuclear tests.
Saying this
made me feel safe. I
did not breathe the bad dust;
I did not drink the fallout water
or eat the contaminated fruit.

I thought: *Tu est moi:*
you are Poma na Vaharoi;
everything will be all right.
I gave a sidelong glance
at brown feet in flip-flops,
crossed brown ankles, creased khaki,
bright flower prints;
at the folded brown hands
of Haamemu Taputuara the fisherman
and Hapaitaha Terii the teacher,
of the young bride, Torohia,
lying still in their laps.

I knew it was a moment of great *mana,*
as if all the stars had lined up
to spell a single word.
Why should it be my aunt
or my *ohana,*
or me, or anyone?
How many will die
on the *manae* of progress?
Will our names be remembered?
Tests all over
the atolls hold us all
together now, make us all one.
There is no clear cause-effect evidence.
Yet there are irradiated iodine therapies,
thyroid hormones, annual chest x-rays.
There are bougainvillea bouquets on white stone.
There is the overheard cry of pain
from a whispering voice which once warbled.
The waiting room was sunny
and air-conditioned. The air conditioner
droned, droned. *The wind*
will blow the wrong way . . .
Toapere's voice
strains around the lump in her throat . . .
The wrong way . . . The wrong way . . .

Then I was awake.
Marura Raiarii,
whose taro field borders
our yams, walked in.
Ia orana, Poma, he greeted me,
in his diminished voice.
We touched cheeks,
kissing the poisoned air.

THE MOHEMBO ROAD

Meditations on a road trip with Abba Jacob
in Botswana and Namibia, 2008

I

People walking. People walking. A fringe
along the road of people on the move.
Adults flagged down rides, tattered children waved.
J. and I on the road left a wake of change.
Free-range cattle and goats—wealth on the hoof—
foraged sparse green, wary of predators
and prowling four-wheel-drive, self-guided tours
catching them in digital photographs.
And donkeys, apparently eager for the chance
to enter green pastures by being killed,
thousands of donkeys. They seemed to be stoned
or grief-stunned: heads down, staring, donkeys stood
in the sun-scorched road, as if trying to recall
the one truth which makes Africa make sense.

II

A one truth by which Africa makes sense?
The continent is the Rosetta Stone,
which explains humanity's origin.
(Though all life is stardust drifted from long-dead suns.)
Africans know this present moment is all
we have or need, past and future but a myth
invented to disguise the simpler truth
pairing oblivion and miracle.
Long, long ago, only Ostrich possessed fire.
He hid it in a pouch under his wing,
keeping the dark secret of cooking meat.
Man tricked him with a lie, and stole fire's power.
Drummers in the villages every evening
celebrate Man's triumph, deep into night.

III

We celebrate Man's triumph over the night,
although no triumph comes without its cost.
In the light from each watt, how many stars are lost?
We devour the future, producing speed and light.
The epidemic of global progress
infects us with insatiable desire,
while decreasing our ability to share.
We spread the virus to villages we pass.
When we pick up hitchhikers, worlds collide
between back seat and front, have-nots and haves.
Dropped at their destinations, they disappear
into our fading memory of a road.
And we drive on in our islanded lives,
travelers encased in artificial air.

IV

Travelers encased in artificial air
look down on the planet, a jewel against the vast.
We reflect light already in the past.
Are we Gaia, one breathing atmosphere?
Are we one undulating school of fish,
or fish with individuality?
The planet clamors with our *me, me, me:*
my name, *my* pain, *my* dream, *my* love, *my* wish.
Can we bow to compassion? What great good
we might make if we willed a larger will,
submerging *self* to find ourselves alone
in full communion: each hair of each head
accounted for. *I cannot be fulfilled*
if you are not fulfilled. For we are one.

V

We are most fulfilled when we know we are one.
Though we're eight billion, and each a tree of life.

We forget too easily how we exist:
like a moving lake face dappled by the sun.
The Mohembo ferry had received five vehicles
full of white tourists, and one police van.
Last came the piled-high cart of a poor man,
pulled by two donkeys, one large and one small,
yoked together by a rope around their necks.
Seeing the river under the gangplank,
they balked, afraid or stubborn. He went wild
with embarrassed rage, and beat them with a stick.
Braying and rearing, they fell overboard and sank.
They were swept downstream, food for the crocodiles.

VI

Swept downstream to be food for crocodiles,
tethered by stupid human cruelty,
those donkeys died because they were not free.
Theirs was a mutuality that kills.
There is another mutuality,
which binds us together with freely chosen love,
which doesn't kill us, but makes us more alive,
enriched by our shared responsibility.
The young Herero in traditional
cow-horn-shaped headwrap and ankle-length gown,
whose swaddled infant cooed up at her face.
The Tswana with her plastic buckets full
of fruits. Boys hitching to a match in town.
Back seat and front seat: an iota whirling in space.

VII

Our fate, on this iota whirling in space,
is to race across this bridge burning at our heels.
To cross it, or to feed the crocodiles.
Some peoples run; some take a slower pace.
Some hadn't made their first steps, until now.
The rule is: *evolve, make money, or die out.*

Take the *!Kung*/San hunter-gatherers: without
land, they are antelope yoked to a plow.
Who will buy their runner's wind, their tracker's eye?
Their necklaces of ostrich egg shell and seeds?
For a reverent kill, is cornmeal a fair exchange?
If one sells a born-free heart, what can one buy?
For sale: *the myth of a desert which supplies all needs,*
where no one walks along the highway's fringe.

FOR THE FEAST OF CORPUS CHRISTI

For Perry and Debbie

Songbirds skitter among the rafters,
scissoring in and out of the high stained windows.
Abba Jacob watches them a moment,
fingering through his tousled hair.
He looks at the gathered waiting,
cocks his head, smiles.

Today is the feast day of the mewling newborn in the hay,
the thirsty teacher wiping his brow, the dying man's iron grimace.
Today we celebrate a squalling toddler with a load in his pants,
a runny-nosed five-year-old, a boy with scabbed knees.
We celebrate Jesus, who suffered and died.
Who laughed, who sneezed, who scratched where he itched.
He did not live by bread alone,
but he lived by bread. And he liked
a cool drink of fresh-dipped water
drawn smiling from the well.
He tasted. He saw.
When he stepped out onto a wave his feet got muddy.
He faced forward as we do, with fingers-crossed faith.

Six rows from the door, Amma Mama notices
the island echolessness of the morning's songbirds.
She'd never dreamed, though she'd always somehow known,
she'd be here again, watching him spacegaze as he speaks.
Hearing him laugh. He described last night's dinner wine
as "masculine," explained that its taste was what
every man would like to be:
intelligent, handsome, reliable, and a little bit rough
around the edges. His voice, she thinks,
is almost sweeter than the birdsong.

As his body, the church, we remember
ourselves in our Eucharist,
giving thanks for the assurance

that we shall not end here.
Trekking through the desert of brevity toward this
shimmering Zion,
is it bread we eat, or manna?
Wine we drink, or dew?
We make Eucharist for the daily miracles
which sustain us: for food, drink, and fellowship,
for the promise of Christ.

The pause fills with twitter. Beyond faint surf,
vast silence.
Abba Jacob raises his eyebrows, shrugs.
If we are the body of Christ,
then our bodies are Christ's bodies, too, *non?*
Your bodies, mine.
A thousand years ago, exiled for his writings,
St. Simeon continued to describe indwelling light.
If we truly love Christ, he wrote, we *inhabit* Christ.
Every part of us, even the most secret, the parts we hide in shame,
every part becomes his, and is therefore healed, hallowed, beautiful
and radiant with loving light. When that happens everything we see
we see gently, every word we speak listens, every act is reverent,
every caress is a blessing.

Around Amma Mama backs straighten, heads slowly nod.
His darklit eyes beacon the pews.
Those of you who have partners, who have vowed
a love without ceasing, when you lie together, make love
to the immeasurable mystery of spirit enfleshed.
Touch each other with Christ's touch.
Kiss each other with Christ's mouth.
Give to and receive from each other Christ's body.
your fingers a sacrament of tenderness.

Blessing air pocked with gasps,
Abba Jacob says *Amen.*

HOW TO BE HUMAN NOW

Written in collaboration with Father Jacques de Foïard Brown ("Abba Jacob")

To discover how to be human now
is the reason we follow the star.
　　　　　　—W. H. Auden

THE CONTEMPLATIVE LIFE

Abba Jacob said:
Contemplation is both the highest act
of being human, and humanity's highest language.
If the language of things reaches beyond things
to designate the Absolute,
the silent interior mantra
bespeaks a profound communion
with that Someone further than ourselves—
and communion within
ourselves, for the two go together.
When we meditate, we enter
paschal mystery, the frontier between death and life.
Egyptian mythology has a wonderful image
of the pass from life to death: a great ship
which bears us to eternity. Charon
is the great passer of Greek mythology,
helping souls cross the River Styx from life to death.
Christianity turns it around: Christ
is the greatest passer, helping us pass
from death to life.
But contemplative life always makes the passage
from death to life, from humanity to divinity.
It always takes the risk of being human.

There is an extraordinary message from the grave
as to what it takes to be human: a letter
from a Cistercian monk, one of seven
who had their throats cut
by Muslim fundamentalist terrorists

in their monastery in the mountains of Algeria
about ten years ago. Their Prior
left a letter, just in case:
they knew it was probably coming,
they knew they were in great risk.
The letter was found and published.
Here is how it ends:

To the one who will have killed me:

and also you, Friend of my final moment,
who would not be aware
of what you are doing,
yet, this: Thank you.
And adieu to you.
For in you, too,
I see the face of God.

Abba Jacob wiped his eyes.
Interval of birdsong from the veranda.

He's seeing not an abstract God,
but a God who has assumed a face,
a God who shows him this face
in every one of those Muslim brothers and sisters,
including the one who kills him.

Contemplative life has no frontiers.
And it is the heritage of all humanity.
Through contemplation we enter
into communion with everybody.
And this leads to service.
But that's a subject
for another day.

THE LANGUAGE OF THE ABSOLUTE

Abba Jacob said:
We talked earlier about celebrating life

in a disenchanted world; about how
to enchant the world again.
Part of reenchantment comes
from being attentive to our senses,
living in this momentary world
attuned to its everyday texture:
how it looks, smells, sounds, tastes, feels.
But we must be attentive to and,
at the same time,
detached from sensory experience.
Things have value in themselves,
but they are signs of something else.
Words and things are always leading us on,
always talking about something beyond themselves.
Things are not a cul-de-sac.
They speak the language of signs,
the language of the Absolute.

STONE ADZE

Abba Jacob said:
We must respect people, of course,
but we must also respect objects, things:
the work of one's own hands, or of others.

Even half-dead dusty objects like those
in a museum deserve respect.
An ancient stone adze
can practically glow
with the patina of age.
We must respect how it weighed in the hands,
what its work meant.
As we respect the patina of life on faces,
we must respect the patina of craftsmanship
on things like furniture or artifacts,
the patina of use on tools.

THE RISK UNTO DEATH

Abba Jacob said:
When you give a gift, you take a risk—
your gift may not be reciprocated,
perhaps it will be refused.
There must be
an element of gratuitousness in every gift.
If it's not reciprocated . . . ?
Well, it's just not.
That's the risk of generosity.

And the risk is worth it, even unto death.
Having generosity of heart,
you need not fear those who kill the body.

TRUTH AND BEAUTY

Abba Jacob said:
Nothing is too good to be true.

LA GARE CENTRAL

Abba Jacob said:
To be human is to be always arriving
and leaving. This place, this person, this day,
this body, this life. Each of us is *La Gare Centrale,*
welcoming arrivals
and waving farewell, farewell, farewell, farewell . . .

WHERE HUMANITY BEGINS

Abba Jacob said:
Perhaps our humanity begins
in receiving the consolation
of the ordinary.
So many people wish to find God
in some parallel world outside or beyond

this one.
We do not need to search for God.
We need to be open to this world
of pain and beauty. It is in our attentiveness
to this broken world
that God
finds us.

NOTHING STRANGER

Abba Jacob said:
To be human is to be a stranger
and at the same time *not* a stranger.
It is to be profoundly involved in the cosmos:
to know that the building blocks of the universe
and your building blocks are the same. It is to be aware
of the community of all life, to bear cosmic consciousness,
to know that we have received
our building blocks as a gift
from the rest of what is alive.
And what is alive is born of stars,
and of the orbits of stars and planets,
their extraordinary explosions and implosions,
dust storms of the universe coming together
to make suns and planets
and comets made almost entirely of water
falling like rain upon a barren planet
in extraordinary outbursts of vapor,
condensing into oceans, and—
life!

FROM "ADVENTURE-MONK!"

In which Abba Jacob is revealed as a monk with a past.

I

History has a way of playing tricks
on those who chase it. Abba Jacob tried
to live at the crossroads, seeking to look
into neither the future nor the past.
Each breath is a significant bingo,
each moment cause for thanks. A courier
handed him a manila envelope
and roared away on the track through the cane,
leaving him standing with his eyebrows raised.
Shrugging, he tossed it on his cluttered desk.
He returned to the rhythmic timelessness,
the ancient mystic power, of manual work.
Gravity answers a lot of questions,
like *Where the bleep did that envelope go?*
which he asked later, after the phone call.
At last he found it in the curls of dust
under his desk, and opened it to find
an airplane ticket and typed instructions.

II

The wind blowing against his back was hot
and filled with fiercely stinging grains of sand.
He'd brought only the bare necessities:
the habit he wore, blankets, a canteen,
one of his passports, and his book of prayer.
Waiting alone in the desert village,
he had no expectations, only trust
and the mantra, constant as his heartbeat.
He looked at the surrounding ragged hills
knowing there would be no escape for him
from the intelligence work in his past.
They'd found him even in his hermitage,

and flown him here. So he'd never be free:
never be free of that violent past,
free of the spy's godless identity.
He'd always turn the prayer book's pages with
a trigger finger. He'd never forget,
nor be forgotten by the Agency.

III

Brown children whispered, and giggled at him;
brown adults passed, making no eye contact
with the strange robed man who sat silently
in the shade under an acacia tree.
Toward evening a jeep stopped. A man got out,
jangling and clanking with survival gear.
He was a white man who'd weathered tempests,
his face bronzed, his dark hair in a buzz cut,
his eyes burning with determination.
"Hello, Jack." Abba Jacob shook his head.
He stood, ignoring the extended hand.
"That's finished, Commander. I'm a new man.
I live a life of solitude and prayer.
I can't go back. I won't." The older man
snorted. "All those years of intense training?
You think the Agency will let you go?
We need you, Jack. Get in the car. Let's talk."
Abba Jacob climbed in, lifting his skirts.

IV

Returning Abba Jacob's nod of thanks,
the server left the room and closed the door,
leaving a tray of bottles and glasses.
The Commander poured himself a healthy shot
of scotch. Abba Jacob gestured *no thanks*.
"I've missed you, Jack. How long will you persist
in this charade? Stop punishing yourself!
They pushed that kid out! It wasn't your fault!

Your penance is a luxury we can't
afford! The world's spinning out of control.
The rifts between us are growing deeper;
religion is a relic of the past.
People yowl in a spiritual void,
like cannibals crying out for meaning.
Evil exists, Jack; real evil exists.
Surely your God would want you to come back
out of your self-imposed exile, to work
with the Agency on the side of good."

V

Shielding their eyes against the cloud of sand
raised by the rotor wash, the two men walked
toward the helicopter. Then one man clapped
his hand to his arm, and fell to his knees.
The robed one pulled him up, helped him aboard,
and saw three gunmen shooting as they rose
out of range into the cloudless blue sky.
"How bad are you shot, Sir?" Abba Jacob
asked, ripping his white habit into strips
to make a tourniquet or bind a wound.
"It's just a skin wound. I was barely grazed.
But thanks: I guess you saved my life again.
Good thing you were wearing those khaki shorts.
Without the habit, you look like a man!
Sorry: I didn't . . . You know what I mean."
White cloth fluttered from Abba Jacob's hand
and through the open door into the sky.
Abba Jacob was looking at the clouds.

VI

"Listen, Jack: they believe there's nothing wrong
with killing babies. They will hide among
school children. They'll use pregnant human shields.
We need new weapons, not just bombs and guns.

That's where you come in." Abba Jacob smiled.
"You don't need weapons; you need miracles.
I'm through with the killing; through with the hate.
I've stripped off that old self. You don't believe,
so this may make no sense to you, but I'm
reborn forgiven, in the death of Christ."
Around them, cutlery clinked porcelain.
Abba Jacob drained his glass in one gulp.
"Tell them I want to fly home tomorrow."
Waiting on the sidewalk for the valet,
the two men stood in silence. Suddenly
a car rounded the corner, the barrels of
automatic weapons in its windows.
Staccato bursts of gunfire filled the night.

       to be continued . . .